BEYOND THE VEIL

A METAPHYSICAL ODYSSEY

KAMIL IDRIS

First published in Great Britain in 2025

Copyright © Kamil Idris

The moral right of the author has been asserted.

All rights reserved.

No part of this publication may be reproduced, stored in a retrieval system, or transmitted, in any form or by any means, without the prior permission in writing of the publisher, nor be otherwise circulated in any form of binding or cover other than that in which it is published and without a similar condition including this condition being imposed on the subsequent purchaser.

Editing, design, typesetting and publishing by UK Book Publishing.

www.ukbookpublishing.com

ISBN: 978-1-917329-55-2

Prologue

In the vast and intricate tapestry of the universe, humanity has always been driven by an insatiable curiosity to understand the forces that govern existence. This quest for knowledge transcends mere scientific inquiry, delving into the realms of metaphysics and spirituality. Our forebears gazed at the stars, pondered the mysteries of life, and sought to uncover the hidden truths that lie beyond the veil of the physical world. This pursuit is not merely academic; it is a profound journey of the soul, an odyssey that seeks to comprehend the unseen power that orchestrates the cosmos with precision, justice, and discipline.

"Beyond the Veil: A Metaphysical Odyssey" is an ambitious endeavour to explore these profound truths, drawing upon the timeless wisdom of the Quran as our primary testimony. The Quran, with its rich tapestry of verses and profound insights, offers a unique lens through which we can view the universe. It invites us to reflect upon the signs of Allah SWT in the natural world, to ponder the intricate balance of creation, and to seek a deeper understanding of our place within this grand design.

As we embark on this metaphysical journey, we will traverse the realms of philosophy, theology, and science, weaving together a coherent narrative that unveils the existence of an unseen power. This power, we argue, is not an abstract concept but a tangible reality, manifesting through the disciplined laws of nature, the moral fabric of human society, and the intricate order of the cosmos. Our exploration will be anchored in the Quranic worldview, which provides a comprehensive framework for understanding the metaphysical dimensions of existence.

This journey is not just about intellectual discovery; it is about spiritual awakening. It is about recognizing the divine signs that permeate every aspect of our lives and understanding how they point to a higher reality. It is about seeing beyond the veil of the material world and perceiving the profound truths that lie beneath. By examining the interplay of justice, discipline, and mercy in the universe, we aim to present a compelling case for the divine orchestration of all that exists.

The chapters that follow will delve deeply into these themes, each one building upon the last to create a comprehensive picture of a universe governed by unseen power. We will explore the nature of reality, the role of justice and discipline in creation, the metaphysical essence of time and space, and the interplay of free will and divine will. We will contemplate the signs of Allah in nature, the journey of the soul, the metaphysics of morality, and the unseen world of angels and jinn. We will reflect on the concepts of divine mercy and ultimate reality, the role of prophethood, and the Quran as a metaphysical guide.

Our aim is to provide a thorough and nuanced exploration of these topics, grounded in the Quranic perspective but enriched by philosophical and scientific insights. We hope to illuminate the profound connections between the seen and unseen, the material and the spiritual, the finite and the infinite. By doing so, we seek to inspire a deeper appreciation of the divine order and a greater sense of connection with the Creator.

"Beyond the Veil: A Metaphysical Odyssey" is an invitation to embark on a journey of discovery and reflection. It is an invitation to look beyond the surface of things and to perceive the deeper realities that lie beneath. It is an invitation to explore the profound wisdom of the Quran and to see how it can guide us towards a more comprehensive understanding of the universe and our place within it. May this journey be a source of enlightenment and inspiration, leading us towards a greater appreciation of the unseen power that governs all existence.

Contents

Prologue iii

Introduction vii

Chapter 1: The Quest for Meaning 1

Chapter 2: The Nature of Reality 7

Chapter 3: The Concept of Justice in the Universe 13

Chapter 4: The Role of Discipline in Creation 21

Chapter 5: The Metaphysical Essence of Time
and Space 29

Chapter 6: The Interplay of Free Will and
Divine Will 37

Chapter 7: The Signs of Allah in Nature 45

Chapter 8: The Soul and Its Journey 53

Chapter 9: The Metaphysics of Morality 61

Chapter 10: The Unseen World 69

Chapter 11: The Concept of Divine Mercy 77

Chapter 12: The Ultimate Reality 85

Chapter 13: The Role of Prophethood 93

Chapter 14: The Quran as a Metaphysical Guide 101

Chapter 15: The Interconnectedness of
　　　　　　All Creation 109

Overall Conclusion: The Metaphysical Odyssey 117

Introduction

The quest for understanding the nature of reality and our place within it has been a timeless pursuit, spanning cultures, epochs, and disciplines. From the earliest myths and religious texts to the sophisticated theories of contemporary science and philosophy, humanity has sought to unravel the mysteries of existence, probing the depths of the cosmos and the human soul alike. "Beyond the Veil: A Metaphysical Odyssey" embarks on this profound journey, seeking to bridge the gap between the seen and the unseen, the material and the metaphysical, through the lens of the Quran.

The Intersection of Science, Philosophy, and Faith

Our exploration begins at the intersection of science, philosophy, and faith. These three pillars of human understanding have often been viewed as distinct, if not conflicting, domains. Science, with its empirical rigour, seeks to decode the laws of nature. Philosophy, with its analytical depth, probes the fundamental questions of existence. Faith, with its spiritual insights, provides a moral and metaphysical framework for understanding the divine.

Yet, these domains are not isolated; they are interwoven strands of a single tapestry. The Quran, as a divine revelation, offers a unique perspective that harmonizes these strands, presenting a holistic view of the universe and our place within it. It challenges the materialistic paradigm that dominates contemporary thought, urging us to consider the metaphysical dimensions that underlie the physical world.

The Quranic Worldview

Central to our journey is the Quranic worldview, which posits a reality that is both seen and unseen. The Quran speaks of a cosmos imbued with divine purpose, governed by principles of justice, discipline, and mercy. It calls upon believers to reflect upon the signs of Allah SWT in the natural world, to seek knowledge, and to engage in deep contemplation. This worldview provides a comprehensive framework for understanding the nature of reality, one that integrates empirical observation with spiritual insight.

The Quranic concept of Tawhid, the oneness of Allah, underscores this worldview. Tawhid asserts that there is no division between the physical and metaphysical realms; both are expressions of Allah's singular reality. This principle of unity implies a holistic view of the universe, where every part is interconnected and purposeful.

The Role of Reflection and Contemplation

The Quran places great emphasis on reflection (tafakkur) and contemplation (tadabbur). These practices are not merely intellectual exercises; they are spiritual disciplines that lead to a deeper understanding of the divine order. Verses such as "Do they not reflect upon themselves? Allah created the heavens and the earth and everything between them in truth and for an appointed term" (Quran 30:8) invite believers to ponder the mysteries of creation and their own existence.

Reflection and contemplation help us transcend the superficial understanding of reality, allowing us to perceive the deeper truths that lie beneath. They guide us towards a more profound appreciation of the divine signs that permeate the universe, leading to spiritual awakening and enlightenment.

The Nature of Reality: Seen and Unseen

Our journey into the nature of reality will explore the intricate relationship between the seen and unseen realms. The seen realm encompasses the physical universe, which we can observe and measure. The unseen realm, however, includes the metaphysical dimensions that lie beyond our sensory perception. The Quran frequently references this unseen realm, urging believers to have faith in its existence and to recognize its influence on the physical world.

This duality of reality challenges the materialistic worldview, which limits existence to what can be empirically observed. The Quranic perspective invites us to expand our understanding, to acknowledge the presence of metaphysical forces, and to see the interconnectedness of all things.

The Journey Towards Ultimate Reality

"Beyond the Veil" is not just an intellectual exploration; it is a spiritual journey towards ultimate reality. This journey involves continuous learning, reflection, and growth. It requires us to transcend the limitations of materialism and embrace a holistic understanding of the universe. By contemplating the signs of Allah and recognizing the interconnectedness of all things, we gain insights into the deeper truths that underlie existence.

The ultimate reality, as presented in the Quran, is Allah SWT, the source and sustainer of all existence. This reality is beyond human comprehension, yet intimately connected to every aspect of our lives. The journey towards understanding this ultimate reality is marked by seeking knowledge, engaging in reflection, and cultivating a deep spiritual connection with the Creator.

The Role of Justice and Discipline in Creation

A key theme in our exploration is the role of justice and discipline in the universe. The Quran portrays the cosmos as a manifestation of divine justice, where every aspect of creation is governed by precise and purposeful laws. This divine order reflects the attributes of Allah SWT, who is both Just (Al-Adl) and Wise (Al-Hakim).

The disciplined nature of creation is evident in the natural laws that govern the universe. These laws are not random or chaotic; they are expressions of divine wisdom and justice. By understanding these principles, we gain a deeper appreciation of the divine orchestration that underlies the cosmos.

The Moral and Ethical Dimensions of Reality

The quest for understanding reality is also a moral and ethical journey. The Quran provides a comprehensive moral framework, rooted in the principles of justice, mercy, and compassion. It calls upon believers to act with integrity, to uphold justice, and to strive for the common good. These ethical principles are not separate from our understanding of reality; they are integral to it.

By recognizing the moral dimensions of reality, we align our actions with the divine order. This alignment leads to a more harmonious and fulfilling existence, both individually and collectively. The Quranic worldview thus provides not only a metaphysical understanding of the universe but also a guide for ethical living.

Conclusion: An Invitation to Journey

"Beyond the Veil: A Metaphysical Odyssey" invites readers to embark on a journey of discovery and reflection. It is an invitation to look beyond the surface of things, to perceive the deeper realities that lie beneath, and to embrace a holistic vision of existence. This journey is guided by the timeless wisdom of the Quran, which offers profound insights into the nature of reality and our place within it.

As we delve into the chapters that follow, we will explore the nature of reality, the role of justice and discipline in creation, the interplay of divine will and human agency, and the signs of Allah in the natural world. We will contemplate the metaphysical dimensions of time and space, the journey of the soul, the ethical implications of our actions, and the ultimate reality of Allah SWT.

May this journey inspire a renewed sense of wonder, a deeper appreciation of the divine order, and a greater connection with the Creator. May it lead to intellectual enlightenment, spiritual fulfilment, and a more profound understanding of the universe and our place within it.

CHAPTER 1

The Quest for Meaning

Introduction to the Quest for Meaning

The quest for meaning is an intrinsic part of the human experience. From the dawn of civilization, humans have sought to understand their place in the cosmos, the purpose of their existence, and the forces that govern their lives. This quest has driven countless inquiries, from the philosophical musings of ancient sages to the scientific endeavours of modern researchers. It is a journey that transcends cultural, temporal, and geographical boundaries, uniting humanity in its shared pursuit of truth.

At the heart of this quest lies a fundamental question: What is the nature of reality? This question prompts us to look beyond the physical world and consider the metaphysical dimensions of existence. While science has provided us with remarkable insights into the workings of the natural world, it often leaves us yearning for answers to deeper, more existential questions. What is the ultimate purpose of life? What happens after death? Is there an unseen power that orchestrates the universe?

Historical Perspectives on Metaphysical Inquiries

Throughout history, various cultures and civilizations have sought to answer these profound questions. Ancient Greek philosophers such as Plato and Aristotle grappled with the nature of reality and the existence of a higher power. Plato's theory of forms posited the existence of an unseen, perfect realm that underlies the physical world, while Aristotle's metaphysics explored the concept of a prime mover, an uncaused cause that initiates all motion and change.

In Eastern philosophy, Hinduism and Buddhism offered their own metaphysical perspectives. Hinduism's concept of Brahman, the ultimate reality that pervades all existence, and Buddhism's teachings on the nature of suffering and the path to enlightenment, reflect deep metaphysical inquiries into the nature of existence and the human condition.

In the Islamic tradition, scholars and theologians have long engaged in metaphysical exploration, drawing upon the Quran and Hadith to understand the nature of the divine and the cosmos. Islamic philosophers such as Al-Farabi, Ibn Sina (Avicenna), and Al-Ghazali made significant contributions to metaphysical thought, blending Greek philosophy with Islamic theology to develop a comprehensive understanding of reality.

The Quranic Perspective on the Quest for Meaning

The Quran, the holy book of Islam, provides profound insights into the quest for meaning. It calls upon believers to reflect upon the signs of Allah SWT in the universe, to ponder the mysteries of creation, and to seek a deeper understanding of their place in the cosmos. The Quranic worldview posits that the universe is a manifestation of divine will, governed by principles of justice, discipline, and mercy.

The Quran emphasizes the importance of seeking knowledge and understanding. It encourages believers to use their intellect to contemplate the natural world and recognize the signs of Allah SWT. Verses such as "Indeed, in the creation of the heavens and the earth and the alternation of the night and the day are signs for those of understanding" (Quran 3:190) invite us to reflect upon the order and harmony of the cosmos, recognizing the divine orchestration behind it.

The Human Drive for Transcendence

The quest for meaning is driven by an innate human desire for transcendence. We are not content with mere existence; we seek to understand the higher purpose behind it. This drive for transcendence is evident in our pursuit of knowledge, our creative endeavours, and our spiritual practices. It reflects a longing to connect with something greater than ourselves, to find our place in the grand scheme of things.

This desire for transcendence is not limited to religious or spiritual pursuits. It is also evident in our scientific endeavours, our artistic expressions, and our philosophical inquiries. Science, in its quest to uncover the laws of nature, seeks to understand the underlying order of the universe. Art, in its many forms, seeks to capture the beauty and mystery of existence. Philosophy, in its pursuit of wisdom, seeks to unravel the fundamental questions of life.

The Role of Reflection and Contemplation

Reflection and contemplation are essential components of the quest for meaning. The Quran encourages believers to engage in deep reflection, to ponder the signs of Allah SWT, and to seek a deeper understanding of reality. This process of reflection is not merely an intellectual exercise; it is a spiritual practice that brings us closer to the divine.

In the Islamic tradition, reflection (tafakkur) and contemplation (tadabbur) are highly valued. These practices involve contemplating the verses of the Quran, reflecting upon the natural world, and pondering the mysteries of creation. Through reflection and contemplation, we gain insights into the divine order and recognize the signs of Allah SWT in the universe.

The Interconnectedness of Knowledge and Faith

The quest for meaning is not a solitary pursuit; it is an interconnected journey that blends knowledge and faith. In the Islamic worldview, knowledge (ilm) and faith (iman) are intertwined, each reinforcing the other. The pursuit of knowledge leads to a deeper understanding of the divine, while faith provides the spiritual foundation for seeking truth.

The Quran emphasizes the importance of seeking knowledge, describing it as a path to understanding the divine order. Verses such as "And those who have been given knowledge see that what is revealed to you from your Lord is the truth and guides to the path of the Exalted in Might, the Praiseworthy" (Quran 34:6) highlight the role of knowledge in guiding us towards the truth.

The Universal Nature of the Quest for Meaning

The quest for meaning is a universal journey that transcends cultural, religious, and philosophical boundaries. It is a shared human experience that unites us in our search for truth and understanding. Throughout history, different cultures and civilizations have contributed to this quest, offering diverse perspectives and insights.

In our contemporary world, the quest for meaning continues to be a driving force behind human endeavours. It shapes our scientific research, our philosophical inquiries, our artistic expressions, and our spiritual practices. It reflects our enduring desire to understand the nature of reality and our place within it.

Conclusion: The Beginning of an Odyssey

As we embark on this metaphysical odyssey, we are guided by the timeless wisdom of the Quran and the profound insights of philosophical and scientific inquiry. Our journey is not just an intellectual exploration; it is a spiritual quest that seeks to uncover the deeper truths that lie beyond the veil of the physical world.

In the chapters that follow, we will delve deeper into the nature of reality, exploring the metaphysical dimensions of existence and the divine orchestration of the universe. We will examine the principles of justice, discipline, and mercy that govern the cosmos, and reflect upon the signs of Allah SWT that permeate every aspect of our lives.

This odyssey is an invitation to look beyond the surface of things and perceive the deeper realities that lie beneath. It is an invitation to seek knowledge, to engage in reflection and contemplation, and to connect with the unseen power that governs all existence. May this journey inspire a renewed sense of wonder, a deeper appreciation of the divine order, and a greater connection with the Creator.

CHAPTER 2
The Nature of Reality

Introduction to Reality

The nature of reality is one of the most profound and enduring questions in philosophy, theology, and science. It beckons us to explore the essence of existence, the foundation of the universe, and the unseen forces that shape our lives. Reality, as we perceive it, is a complex interplay of physical phenomena, consciousness, and metaphysical principles. This chapter delves into these intricate layers, drawing from the Quranic worldview to provide a comprehensive understanding of reality's true nature.

The Limitations of Materialism

Materialism, the philosophical stance that asserts that only physical matter exists, has long dominated scientific inquiry. While it has yielded significant insights into the workings of the natural world, materialism often falls short in explaining the deeper aspects of existence. It struggles to account for consciousness, the nature of time, and the metaphysical principles that underlie the cosmos.

The Quran offers a different perspective, one that transcends the limitations of materialism. It presents a reality that is both seen and unseen, a universe imbued with divine purpose and meaning. The Quranic view challenges us to look beyond the material and recognize the signs of Allah SWT in every aspect of creation.

The Seen and Unseen Realms

According to the Quran, reality encompasses both the seen (al-shahada) and the unseen (al-ghayb) realms. The seen realm includes the physical universe that we can observe and measure, while the unseen realm encompasses the metaphysical dimensions that lie beyond our sensory perception. These two realms are intricately connected, each influencing the other in profound ways.

The Quran frequently references the unseen realm, urging believers to have faith in its existence. Verses such as "This is the Book about which there is no doubt, a guidance for those conscious of Allah – who believe in the unseen" (Quran 2:2-3) emphasize the importance of recognizing and believing in the unseen aspects of reality. This belief is not a blind faith but an acknowledgment of the deeper truths that underpin the physical world.

The Metaphysical Framework

The Quran provides a rich metaphysical framework that explains the nature of reality. It posits that Allah SWT is the ultimate reality, the source and sustainer of all existence. Everything in the universe is a manifestation of His will and reflects His attributes. This divine reality is beyond human comprehension, yet it is intimately connected to every aspect of our lives.

The Quranic concept of Tawhid, the oneness of Allah, underscores this framework. It asserts that there is no division between the physical and metaphysical realms; both are expressions of Allah's singular reality. This oneness implies a holistic view of the universe, where every part is interconnected and purposeful.

The Role of Consciousness

Consciousness is a central aspect of reality that materialism struggles to explain. The Quran acknowledges the profound nature of human consciousness, describing it as a gift from Allah that allows us to perceive, reflect, and seek understanding. Consciousness is not merely a byproduct of physical processes; it is a divine endowment that connects us to the metaphysical realm.

The Quran encourages believers to use their consciousness to contemplate the signs of Allah in the universe. Verses such as "Do they not reflect upon themselves? Allah created the heavens and the earth and everything between them in truth and for an appointed term. Yet many people deny they will meet their Lord" (Quran 30:8) highlight the importance of reflection and self-awareness in understanding the nature of reality.

The Nature of Time and Space

Time and space are fundamental dimensions of reality, yet their true nature remains elusive. The Quran offers insights into these dimensions, portraying them as creations of Allah that serve specific purposes. Time is described as a means for humans to measure their lives and actions, while space is the expanse in which creation unfolds.

The Quranic view of time and space transcends the linear, mechanistic understanding of modern science. It presents a dynamic, purposeful reality where time and space are interwoven with divine will. Verses such as "He created the heavens and earth in truth. He wraps the night over the day and wraps the day over the night and has subjected the sun and the moon, each running [its course] for a specified term. Unquestionably, He is the Exalted in Might, the Perpetual Forgiver" (Quran 39:5) illustrate this profound interconnectedness.

The Interplay of Divine Will and Human Agency

A key aspect of reality in the Quranic framework is the interplay between divine will and human agency. The Quran asserts that while Allah is the ultimate orchestrator of the universe, humans are endowed with free will to make choices and shape their destinies. This duality is a central theme in understanding the nature of reality.

The Quran presents life as a test, where human actions and choices are significant and consequential. Verses such as "Indeed, this is a reminder, so whoever wills may take to his Lord a way. But you will not will unless Allah wills. Indeed, Allah is ever Knowing and Wise" (Quran 76:29-30) highlight the balance between divine will and human freedom. This interplay underscores the moral and ethical dimensions of reality, where humans are accountable for their actions.

The Signs of Allah in Creation

The Quran invites us to contemplate the signs of Allah in the natural world as a means to understand the deeper aspects of reality. These signs (ayat) are evident in the order, beauty, and complexity of the universe. They serve as reminders of Allah's presence and attributes, guiding us towards a deeper appreciation of the divine reality.

Verses such as "Indeed, in the creation of the heavens and the earth and the alternation of the night and the day are signs for those of understanding – who remember Allah while standing or sitting or [lying] on their sides and give thought to the creation of the heavens and the earth, [saying], 'Our Lord, You did not create this aimlessly; exalted are You [above such a thing]; then protect us from the punishment of the Fire'" (Quran 3:190-191) emphasize the importance of reflection on the natural world. These signs are not merely physical phenomena; they are manifestations of divine wisdom and purpose.

The Journey Towards Ultimate Reality

The quest to understand the nature of reality is a journey towards recognizing and connecting with the ultimate reality, Allah SWT. This journey involves both intellectual inquiry and spiritual awakening. The Quran guides us on this path, providing a comprehensive framework that integrates knowledge and faith.

The journey towards ultimate reality is marked by continuous learning, reflection, and growth. It requires us to transcend the limitations of materialism and embrace a holistic understanding of the universe. By contemplating the signs of Allah and recognizing the interconnectedness of all things, we gain insights into the deeper truths that underlie existence.

Conclusion: A Unified Vision of Reality

The nature of reality, as presented in the Quran, is a unified vision that encompasses both the seen and unseen realms. It is a reality imbued with divine purpose, governed by principles of justice, discipline, and mercy. This vision challenges the materialistic paradigm, offering a more comprehensive and meaningful understanding of existence.

As we continue our metaphysical odyssey, we are called to reflect on the signs of Allah, to seek knowledge and understanding, and to connect with the ultimate reality that underlies the cosmos. This journey is not merely an intellectual pursuit; it is a path towards spiritual fulfilment and a deeper appreciation of the divine order.

May this exploration inspire us to look beyond the surface of things, to recognize the deeper truths that lie beneath, and to embrace a holistic vision of reality that honours both the seen and unseen dimensions of existence.

CHAPTER 3

The Concept of Justice in the Universe

Introduction to Divine Justice

The notion of justice is fundamental to understanding the divine order of the universe. In human societies, justice serves as a cornerstone for morality, law, and governance. However, the concept of justice extends far beyond human constructs; it is deeply embedded in the very fabric of the cosmos. The Quran presents justice as a central attribute of Allah SWT, reflecting His perfect wisdom and balance in creation. This chapter delves into the multifaceted nature of divine justice, exploring its manifestations in the natural and moral order of the universe, as well as its profound implications for human existence.

The Quranic Foundation of Justice

The Quran provides a comprehensive framework for understanding justice, both in its theological and practical dimensions. The Arabic term for justice, "Adl", encompasses notions of balance, fairness, and equity. Allah SWT is often described as "Al-Adl" (The Just), emphasizing that His actions and decrees are rooted in perfect justice.

Numerous Quranic verses highlight the centrality of justice in the divine order. For instance, Allah states, "Indeed, Allah commands you to render trusts to whom they are due and when you judge between people to judge with justice" (Quran 4:58). This verse underscores the divine mandate for justice in human interactions, reflecting a broader cosmic principle that governs all creation.

Justice in the Natural Order

The natural world is a testament to the principle of divine justice. The intricate laws of physics, chemistry, and biology reflect a harmonious balance that sustains life and the cosmos. These laws operate with precision, ensuring that the universe functions in an orderly and predictable manner.

The Quran invites believers to reflect upon the signs of justice in the natural world. Verses such as "And the heaven He raised and imposed the balance" (Quran 55:7) and "It is He who created the night and the day and the sun and the moon; each in an orbit floating" (Quran 21:33) highlight the meticulous balance and order that characterize creation. This balance is not accidental but a manifestation of Allah's justice, ensuring that every element of the universe operates within its ordained limits.

The cycles of nature, such as the changing seasons, the water cycle, and the food chain, further exemplify this justice. Each component of these cycles plays a vital role in maintaining ecological equilibrium. Disruptions to this balance, often caused by human actions, lead to environmental degradation, underscoring the importance of adhering to the principles of justice in our stewardship of the Earth.

Justice in the Moral and Social Order

Justice is equally paramount in the moral and social order. The Quranic concept of justice extends to all aspects of human life, including interpersonal relationships, economic transactions, and legal judgments. The Quran calls upon believers to uphold justice, even when it is difficult or against their own interests. "O you who have believed, be persistently standing firm in justice, witnesses for Allah, even if it be against yourselves or parents and relatives" (Quran 4:135).

The moral dimensions of justice are reflected in the Quranic injunctions against oppression, dishonesty, and exploitation. Allah SWT commands fairness in trade, honesty in testimony, and compassion towards the vulnerable. These principles are designed to create a just and harmonious society, where individuals are treated with dignity and their rights are protected.

One of the most profound expressions of justice in the Quran is the concept of retributive justice, where individuals are held accountable for their actions. This principle is encapsulated in the verse, "And We have made every man's actions cling to his neck, and We will bring forth to him on the Day of Resurrection a book which he will find wide open. 'Read your book; your soul suffices today as a reckoner against you'" (Quran 17:13-14). This verse highlights the ultimate justice of the Hereafter, where every deed is weighed and recompensed accordingly.

The Interplay of Justice and Mercy

While justice is a foundational principle, it is harmoniously balanced with mercy in the Quranic worldview. Allah SWT is described as both "Al-Adl" (The Just) and "Ar-Rahman" (The Most Merciful). This duality reflects a divine balance, where justice is tempered with compassion and forgiveness.

The interplay of justice and mercy is evident in the Quranic narrative of human creation and divine guidance. Allah SWT's justice demands accountability for actions, while His mercy provides opportunities for repentance and redemption. Verses such as "Say, 'O My servants who have transgressed against themselves [by sinning], do not despair of the mercy of Allah. Indeed, Allah forgives all sins. Indeed, it is He who is the Forgiving, the Merciful'" (Quran 39:53) illustrate this profound balance.

Divine Justice and Human Free Will

A critical aspect of understanding divine justice is its relationship with human free will. The Quran affirms that humans are endowed with the capacity to choose their actions, and they are held accountable for their choices. This accountability is a cornerstone of divine justice, ensuring that individuals are rewarded or punished based on their deeds.

The Quranic perspective on free will and divine justice is encapsulated in the verse, "And say, 'The truth is from your Lord, so whoever wills – let him believe; and whoever wills – let him disbelieve. Indeed, We have prepared for the wrongdoers a fire whose walls will surround them. And if they call for relief, they will be relieved with water like murky oil, which scalds [their] faces. Wretched is the drink, and evil is the resting place'" (Quran 18:29). This verse underscores the moral agency of humans and the consequences of their choices.

Justice as a Path to Social Harmony

The Quranic vision of justice is not limited to individual conduct; it extends to the broader social and political order. Justice is seen as a means to achieve social harmony and cohesion. A just society is one where the rights of all individuals are upheld, and where laws are applied fairly and equitably.

The Quran advocates for social justice through various injunctions, including the fair distribution of wealth, the protection of the weak and vulnerable, and the establishment of fair legal systems. Zakat (almsgiving), one of the Five Pillars of Islam, is a practical manifestation of social justice, aimed at reducing economic inequality and supporting those in need.

The Quran also emphasizes the importance of justice in leadership and governance. Leaders are urged to rule with fairness and integrity, and to avoid tyranny and corruption. The verse, "O David, indeed We have made you a successor upon the earth, so judge between the people in truth and do not follow [your] desire, as it will lead you astray from the way of Allah" (Quran 38:26), highlights the responsibility of rulers to uphold justice and avoid personal biases.

The Eschatological Dimension of Justice

The ultimate manifestation of divine justice is in the eschatological vision of the Quran. The Day of Judgment is depicted as a time when all individuals will be held accountable for their deeds, and justice will be perfectly realized. This eschatological justice is a central theme in the Quran, providing both a warning and a hope for believers.

On the Day of Judgment, every deed, no matter how small, will be weighed and judged. Verses such as "So whoever does an atom's weight of good will see it, and whoever does an atom's weight of evil will see it" (Quran 99:7-8) emphasize the meticulous and comprehensive nature of divine justice. This ultimate reckoning assures believers that justice will be served, even if it is not fully realized in this worldly life.

The Spiritual Significance of Justice

Justice is not only a legal and social principle; it has profound spiritual significance. Upholding justice is an act of worship, reflecting the believer's commitment to the divine order. It aligns the human will with the will of Allah SWT, fostering a deeper connection with the Creator.

The pursuit of justice requires humility, patience, and courage. It involves standing up for the truth, even in the face of adversity, and striving to rectify injustices in one's own life and in society. By embodying the principles of justice, believers cultivate a sense of integrity and righteousness, drawing closer to Allah SWT.

Conclusion: Embracing Divine Justice

The concept of justice in the Quran is multifaceted, encompassing the natural, moral, social, and eschatological dimensions of reality. It is a reflection of Allah's perfect wisdom and balance, manifesting in every aspect of creation. Understanding and embracing this divine justice is essential for achieving a harmonious and fulfilling existence.

As we continue our metaphysical odyssey, we are called to reflect upon the profound principles of justice that govern the universe. By recognizing the signs of Allah's justice in the natural world, upholding justice in our personal and social lives, and preparing for the ultimate justice of the Hereafter, we align ourselves with the divine order. This alignment leads to spiritual growth, ethical integrity, and a deeper appreciation of the divine orchestration that underlies all existence.

CHAPTER 4

The Role of Discipline in Creation

Introduction to Divine Discipline

The concept of discipline is integral to understanding the order and harmony that characterize the universe. In human experience, discipline often refers to self-control, adherence to rules, and the structured pursuit of goals. However, when applied to the divine realm, discipline transcends these mundane definitions. It encompasses the precise and purposeful orchestration of all creation by Allah SWT. This chapter explores the multifaceted nature of divine discipline, examining its manifestations in the natural world, its theological implications, and its profound impact on human life.

The Quranic Foundation of Discipline

The Quran provides a rich tapestry of verses that highlight the disciplined nature of creation. The Arabic term for discipline, "Nizam," implies order, structure, and harmony. Allah SWT is described as the ultimate orchestrator, who has set everything in its proper place with meticulous precision. The Quran states, "He who created the seven heavens in layers. You do not see in the creation of the Most Merciful any inconsistency. So return your vision to the sky, do you see any breaks?" (Quran 67:3).

This verse invites believers to reflect on the seamless order of the universe, emphasizing that there are no flaws or inconsistencies in Allah's creation. The disciplined nature of the cosmos is a testament to Allah's perfect wisdom and power, demonstrating that everything operates according to divine will and purpose.

The Discipline of Natural Laws

The natural world operates under a set of laws that ensure consistency and predictability. These laws, which govern everything from the motion of celestial bodies to the behaviour of subatomic particles, reflect the disciplined nature of creation. The Quran repeatedly emphasizes the precision and regularity of these laws, as seen in verses such as, "It is He who created the night and the day and the sun and the moon; each in an orbit floating" (Quran 21:33).

The regularity of natural phenomena, such as the rising and setting of the sun, the cycles of the moon, and the changing seasons, are all manifestations of divine discipline. These phenomena operate with unwavering precision, providing a stable and orderly environment for life to flourish. The Quran encourages believers to contemplate these signs, recognizing the disciplined hand of Allah behind them.

The Interconnectedness of Creation

One of the most profound aspects of divine discipline is the interconnectedness of all creation. The universe is not a collection of isolated entities, but a harmonious web of relationships and interactions. The Quran highlights this interconnectedness, stating, "And We have created from water every living thing. Then will they not believe?" (Quran 21:30).

This verse underscores the unity and interdependence of all life forms, which are sustained by a common element – water. This interconnectedness extends to the broader cosmos, where the laws of nature ensure that every component of the universe functions in harmony with the rest. The balance of ecosystems, the cycles of matter and energy, and the intricate relationships within biological communities all exemplify the disciplined order of creation.

Discipline in Human Life

Just as the natural world operates under divine discipline, human life is also governed by principles of order and structure. The Quran provides comprehensive guidance on how to live a disciplined life, encompassing aspects such as worship, morality, and social conduct. Verses like, "And establish prayer and give zakah and bow with those who bow [in worship and obedience]" (Quran 2:43), highlight the importance of regular worship and adherence to ethical principles.

Discipline in worship involves regular prayers, fasting, and other acts of devotion that strengthen the believer's connection with Allah. These practices instil a sense of order and routine, fostering spiritual growth and self-discipline. The disciplined nature of Islamic worship is a reflection of the broader cosmic order, aligning human actions with the divine will.

The Moral and Ethical Dimensions of Discipline

Divine discipline also encompasses the moral and ethical dimensions of human life. The Quran provides clear guidelines on ethical behaviour, emphasizing principles such as honesty, justice, and compassion. These ethical principles are not arbitrary; they are rooted in the disciplined order of creation and reflect the divine attributes of Allah.

The disciplined adherence to moral principles is essential for achieving social harmony and individual well-being. The Quran states, "O you who have believed, fear Allah and speak words of appropriate justice. He will [then] amend for you your deeds and forgive you your sins. And whoever obeys Allah and His Messenger has certainly attained a great attainment" (Quran 33:70-71). This verse highlights the importance of disciplined speech and behaviour, promising divine rewards for those who uphold these principles.

The Role of Discipline in Spiritual Growth

Spiritual growth is deeply intertwined with discipline. The Quran emphasizes that a disciplined life leads to greater spiritual awareness and closeness to Allah. Acts of worship, ethical conduct, and self-restraint are all aspects of spiritual discipline that help believers cultivate a deeper connection with the divine.

Fasting during the month of Ramadan is a prime example of spiritual discipline. The Quran states, "O you who have believed, decreed upon you is fasting as it was decreed upon those before you that you may become righteous" (Quran 2:183). Fasting requires abstaining from food, drink, and other physical needs during daylight hours, fostering self-control and heightened spiritual awareness. This disciplined practice is a means of purifying the soul and developing a closer relationship with Allah.

The Discipline of Time and Space

Time and space are fundamental dimensions of existence that are governed by divine discipline. The Quran presents a nuanced understanding of these dimensions, emphasizing their role in the orderly unfolding of creation. Verses such as, "He created the heavens and earth in truth. He wraps the night over the day and wraps the day over the night and has subjected the sun and the moon, each running [its course] for a specified term" (Quran 39:5), highlight the disciplined nature of temporal and spatial cycles.

The disciplined nature of time is evident in the precise alternation of day and night, the regularity of celestial movements, and the passage of seasons. These temporal rhythms provide a framework for human life, influencing daily routines, agricultural practices, and religious observances. The Quran encourages believers to reflect on the disciplined order of time and space, recognizing them as signs of Allah's wisdom and power.

Divine Discipline and Free Will

A key aspect of divine discipline is its relationship with human free will. The Quran affirms that while Allah has ordained a disciplined order for creation, humans are endowed with free will to make choices and shape their destinies. This interplay between divine discipline and human agency is central to understanding the moral and ethical dimensions of life.

The Quranic perspective on free will and discipline is encapsulated in the verse, "And say, 'The truth is from your Lord, so whoever wills – let him believe; and whoever wills – let him disbelieve'" (Quran 18:29). This verse underscores the moral responsibility of humans to choose their path, while acknowledging that their choices are made within the framework of divine discipline. This interplay ensures that human actions are significant and consequential, aligning with the broader order of creation.

The Eschatological Dimension of Discipline

The ultimate manifestation of divine discipline is seen in the eschatological vision of the Quran. The Day of Judgment is depicted as a time when the disciplined order of the universe will be fully realized, and every deed will be accounted for. This eschatological perspective reinforces the importance of living a disciplined life, as it determines one's ultimate fate.

The Quran states, "And the record [of deeds] will be placed [open], and you will see the criminals fearful of that within it, and they will say, 'Oh, woe to us! What is this book that leaves nothing small or great except that it has enumerated it?' And they will find what they did present [before them]. And your Lord does injustice to no one" (Quran 18:49). This verse highlights the meticulous accounting of deeds and the perfect justice of Allah, underscoring the disciplined nature of divine judgment.

The Harmony of Discipline and Mercy

Divine discipline is harmoniously balanced with mercy in the Quranic worldview. While discipline ensures order and justice, mercy provides opportunities for repentance and forgiveness. This balance is beautifully illustrated in the verse, "Say, 'O My servants who have transgressed against themselves [by sinning], do not despair of the mercy of Allah. Indeed, Allah forgives all sins. Indeed, it is He who is the Forgiving, the Merciful'" (Quran 39:53).

This verse emphasizes that despite the disciplined nature of divine order, Allah's mercy is ever-present, offering hope and redemption to those who seek it. The balance of discipline and mercy reflects the comprehensive nature of divine governance, ensuring that justice is tempered with compassion.

Conclusion: Embracing Divine Discipline

The role of discipline in creation, as presented in the Quran, is multifaceted and profound. It encompasses the natural, moral, temporal, and eschatological dimensions of existence, reflecting the perfect wisdom and power of Allah SWT. Understanding and embracing this divine discipline is essential for achieving a harmonious and fulfilling life.

As we continue our metaphysical odyssey, we are called to reflect upon the disciplined order of the universe and align our lives with these principles. By recognizing the signs of divine discipline in the natural world, adhering to ethical and moral guidelines, and striving for spiritual growth, we can cultivate a deeper connection with Allah and live in harmony with His creation. This journey towards understanding divine discipline leads to intellectual enlightenment, spiritual fulfilment, and a greater appreciation of the divine orchestration that underlies all existence.

CHAPTER 5

The Metaphysical Essence of Time and Space

Introduction to Time and Space

Time and space are the fundamental dimensions that structure our existence. They frame the physical universe, influence our perception of reality, and govern the cycles of life. While science provides extensive insights into the mechanics of time and space, the metaphysical dimensions of these concepts remain profound and elusive. This chapter delves into the Quranic perspective on time and space, exploring their deeper meanings, their role in the divine order, and their implications for human existence and spirituality.

The Quranic Concept of Time

The Quran presents a nuanced and multifaceted view of time. It acknowledges the linear progression of time that characterizes human experience, but also introduces the concept of a divine time that transcends human understanding. The Quranic term for time, "Dahr", encompasses both the temporal sequence and the eternal continuum.

One of the most significant Quranic verses about time is, "By time, indeed, mankind is in loss, except for those who have believed and done righteous deeds and advised each other to truth and advised each other to patience" (Quran 103:1-3). This verse highlights the moral and spiritual dimensions of time, emphasizing the importance of utilizing time wisely for righteous deeds and mutual support.

The Relative Nature of Time

The Quranic perspective on time aligns with the modern scientific understanding of its relativity. Einstein's theory of relativity revolutionized our understanding of time, showing that it is not an absolute constant but varies with the speed and gravity. The Quran alludes to this relativity in verses like, "A day with your Lord is like a thousand years of what you count" (Quran 22:47), and, "The angels and the Spirit will ascend to Him during a Day the extent of which is fifty thousand years" (Quran 70:4).

These verses suggest that divine time operates on a different scale than human time, reflecting a more expansive and complex understanding of temporal dimensions. This concept challenges us to broaden our perception of time, recognizing that the divine perspective encompasses both the fleeting moments of human life and the vast epochs of cosmic history.

The Cyclical Nature of Time

In addition to its linear progression, the Quran also presents time as cyclical, mirroring the recurring patterns found in nature. The cycles of day and night, the phases of the moon, and the changing seasons are all reflections of this cyclical nature. The Quran states, "And He has made subject to you the night and day and the sun and moon, and the stars are subjected by His command. Indeed in that are signs for a people who reason" (Quran 16:12).

These cycles provide a rhythm to life, structuring our daily routines, agricultural practices, and religious observances. The cyclical nature of time invites believers to reflect on the recurring patterns of creation, recognizing them as signs of Allah's orderly and purposeful design.

The Concept of Divine Decree and Human Time

The Quran emphasizes that all events unfold according to a divine decree (Qadar), which operates within the framework of time. This decree encompasses every aspect of creation, from the grandest cosmic events to the minutest details of individual lives. The Quran states, "And every small and great [thing] is inscribed" (Quran 54:53), and "No disaster strikes upon the earth or among yourselves except that it is in a register before We bring it into being – indeed that, for Allah, is easy" (Quran 57:22).

The concept of divine decree challenges the linear and deterministic view of time, suggesting that while humans experience time sequentially, Allah's knowledge and will encompass all of time simultaneously. This understanding provides a profound sense of trust and reliance on Allah's wisdom and justice, knowing that every moment and event is part of a greater divine plan.

The Metaphysical Dimensions of Space

Just as the Quran offers a rich understanding of time, it also presents a profound view of space. The Quranic term for space, "Makaan", encompasses both physical locations and metaphysical realms. Space is not merely an empty void; it is a dynamic and purposeful creation that reflects the divine attributes of Allah.

The Quran emphasizes the vastness and intricacy of the cosmos, stating, "Do you not see that Allah has created the heavens and the earth in truth? If He wills, He can do away with you and produce a new creation" (Quran 14:19). This verse highlights the grandeur and scale of the universe, inviting believers to contemplate the expansive nature of creation and its underlying divine purpose.

The Unity of Creation

A central theme in the Quranic perspective on space is the unity and interconnectedness of creation. The universe is not a collection of isolated entities, but a cohesive and interdependent whole. This unity is reflected in verses such as, "It is He who created the heavens and the earth in six days and then established Himself above the Throne. He knows what penetrates into the earth and what emerges from it and what descends from the heaven and what ascends therein; and He is with you wherever you are. And Allah, of what you do, is Seeing" (Quran 57:4).

This verse underscores the omnipresence and omniscience of Allah, highlighting that every part of the universe is connected through divine knowledge and presence. The unity of creation reflects the singular reality of Tawhid, where every element of space is a manifestation of Allah's will and wisdom.

The Sacredness of Space

The Quran also imparts a sense of sacredness to certain spaces, recognizing their spiritual significance. Places of worship, such as mosques, are considered sacred due to their role in facilitating communion with Allah. The Quran states, "The mosques are for Allah, so do not invoke with Allah anyone" (Quran 72:18). This verse underscores the sanctity of places dedicated to worship and spiritual reflection.

Furthermore, the Quran highlights specific locations as sacred, such as the Kaaba in Mecca, which is described as "the first House [of worship] established for mankind" (Quran 3:96). These sacred spaces serve as focal points for spiritual practices, pilgrimage, and communal worship, reinforcing the connection between physical locations and metaphysical realities.

The Concept of Barzakh

The Quran introduces the concept of Barzakh, an intermediate realm that exists between the physical world and the Hereafter. Barzakh is often described as a barrier or partition that separates different states of existence. The Quran states, "And behind them is a barrier until the Day they are resurrected" (Quran 23:100).

Barzakh represents a metaphysical space where souls reside after death and before the final judgment. It highlights the continuity of existence beyond physical life, emphasizing that space transcends the material world. This concept encourages believers to reflect on the transient nature of physical existence and the enduring reality of the soul.

The Eschatological Transformation of Time and Space

The Quranic eschatology presents a transformative vision of time and space, where the current dimensions of existence will be altered in the Hereafter. The Day of Judgment is depicted as a time when the heavens and the earth will undergo profound changes, reflecting the ultimate fulfilment of divine justice and mercy.

The Quran states, "The Day when the earth will be replaced by another earth, and the heavens [as well], and they [i.e., creatures] will come out before Allah, the One, the Prevailing" (Quran 14:48). This verse suggests that the eschatological transformation will involve a fundamental reconfiguration of time and space, ushering in a new reality that transcends the limitations of the present world.

The Spiritual Significance of Time and Space

The Quranic perspective on time and space has profound spiritual implications. It encourages believers to live with an awareness of the divine presence and purpose that permeates every moment and every place. Time is seen as a precious and finite resource, to be used wisely for spiritual growth, righteous deeds, and the remembrance of Allah. Space is viewed as a dynamic and sacred creation, filled with signs that point to the divine.

The spiritual significance of time is emphasized in the practice of daily prayers (Salah), which structure the day around moments of worship and reflection. The disciplined observance of these prayers fosters a deep sense of connection with Allah and a mindful approach to the passage of time. Similarly, the practice of pilgrimage (Hajj) underscores the spiritual significance of space, as believers travel to sacred locations to perform rituals that symbolize their submission to Allah.

Conclusion: Embracing the Metaphysical Dimensions of Time and Space

The Quranic view of time and space offers a rich and multifaceted understanding that transcends the limitations of materialism. It presents time as both linear and cyclical, relative and eternal, reflecting the divine decree and human agency. Space is depicted as a dynamic and interconnected creation, imbued with sacredness and purpose.

As we continue our metaphysical odyssey, we are called to reflect on the deeper meanings of time and space, recognizing them as signs of Allah's wisdom and power. By embracing the spiritual dimensions of these fundamental concepts, we can cultivate a deeper appreciation of the divine order and align our lives with the greater cosmic purpose. This journey towards understanding the metaphysical essence of time and space leads to intellectual enlightenment, spiritual fulfilment, and a profound connection with the Creator.

CHAPTER 6

The Interplay of Free Will and Divine Will

Introduction to Free Will and Divine Will

The interplay between free will and divine will is a profound and complex theme that has captivated theologians, philosophers, and scholars for centuries. In the Islamic tradition, this interplay is particularly significant, as it addresses the balance between human agency and the overarching sovereignty of Allah SWT. This chapter explores the Quranic perspective on free will and divine will, examining their implications for human responsibility, moral accountability, and the divine plan. By delving into the depths of this intricate relationship, we aim to uncover the profound wisdom that underlies the coexistence of human freedom and divine governance.

The Quranic Foundation of Free Will

The Quran affirms the existence of human free will, emphasizing that individuals are endowed with the capacity to make choices and are held accountable for their actions. This principle is evident in numerous verses that highlight the moral responsibility of human beings. For instance, the Quran states, "And say, 'The truth is from your Lord, so whoever wills – let him believe; and whoever wills – let him disbelieve'" (Quran 18:29). This verse underscores the agency given to individuals to choose their path, whether in belief or disbelief.

The concept of free will is further reinforced by the Quranic portrayal of human beings as moral agents who bear the weight of their decisions. Verses such as "Indeed, We guided him to the way, be he grateful or be he ungrateful" (Quran 76:3) highlight the dual potential within humans to choose gratitude and righteousness or ingratitude and wrongdoing. This duality is a testament to the significance of human choices in shaping one's destiny.

The Nature of Divine Will

While the Quran affirms human free will, it simultaneously emphasizes the supremacy of divine will. Allah SWT is depicted as the ultimate orchestrator of the universe, whose will encompasses all that exists. The Quran states, "And your Lord creates what He wills and chooses; not for them was the choice. Exalted is Allah and high above what they associate with Him" (Quran 28:68). This verse highlights the absolute sovereignty of Allah, who creates and decrees according to His wisdom and purpose.

Divine will, or "Mashi'a", operates on a level that transcends human understanding. It encompasses both the macrocosmic order of the universe and the microcosmic details of individual lives. The Quranic view of divine will is not deterministic in a fatalistic sense but reflects a harmonious balance between divine decree and human agency. This balance ensures that while

Allah's will is paramount, human actions remain meaningful and consequential.

The Balance Between Free Will and Divine Will

The Quranic perspective on the interplay between free will and divine will is best understood through the concept of "Tawakkul" (trust in Allah) and "Qadar" (divine decree). Tawakkul involves trusting in Allah's wisdom and plan, while Qadar refers to the divine decree that shapes the course of events. Together, these concepts illustrate the balanced relationship between human effort and reliance on divine will.

The Quran states, "And whoever relies upon Allah – then He is sufficient for him. Indeed, Allah will accomplish His purpose. Allah has already set for everything a [decreed] extent" (Quran 65:3). This verse encourages believers to place their trust in Allah while recognizing that their actions and efforts are part of the divine plan. The balance between free will and divine will is reflected in the principle that humans must strive to fulfil their responsibilities while trusting in Allah's ultimate control over outcomes.

The Moral and Ethical Implications

The interplay of free will and divine will has profound moral and ethical implications. The Quran emphasizes that human beings are accountable for their choices and actions, which are recorded and judged by Allah. Verses such as "So whoever does an atom's weight of good will see it, and whoever does an atom's weight of evil will see it" (Quran 99:7-8) underscore the meticulous accounting of deeds and the moral responsibility of individuals.

The recognition of divine will does not absolve humans of their ethical duties; rather, it enhances their sense of accountability. The Quran states, "And fear a Day when you will be returned to Allah. Then every soul will be compensated for what it earned, and they will not be wronged" (Quran 2:281). This verse highlights the importance of living a righteous life, knowing that every action will be judged with perfect justice.

The Role of Intention (Niyyah)

In the Quranic framework, intention (Niyyah) plays a crucial role in the interplay between free will and divine will. Intention reflects the inner motivations and purposes behind human actions, and it is a key factor in determining their moral and spiritual value. The Quran states, "And We will regard what they have done of deeds and make them as dust dispersed" (Quran 25:23), indicating that actions devoid of sincere intention are rendered worthless.

The emphasis on intention underscores the significance of aligning one's will with the divine will. Acts performed with the intention of seeking Allah's pleasure are imbued with spiritual merit, even if the outcomes are beyond human control. This principle is beautifully illustrated in the Hadith, "Actions are judged by intentions, and each person will be rewarded according to their intention". This Hadith, reported by Umar ibn Al-Khattab, highlights the centrality of intention in the Islamic ethical framework.

The Wisdom Behind Trials and Tribulations

The Quran teaches that trials and tribulations are part of the divine plan, serving as tests of faith and opportunities for spiritual growth. The interplay between free will and divine will is evident in how individuals respond to these challenges. The Quran states, "Do you think that you will enter Paradise while such [trial] has not yet come to you as came to those who passed on before you? They were touched by poverty and hardship and were shaken until [even their] messenger and those who believed with him said, 'When is the help of Allah?' Unquestionably, the help of Allah is near" (Quran 2:214).

This verse emphasizes that trials are a means of refining and strengthening faith. Believers are encouraged to exercise their free will by responding with patience, perseverance, and trust in Allah's wisdom. The recognition that trials are part of a greater divine plan provides comfort and perspective, helping believers navigate life's challenges with resilience and hope.

The Concept of Divine Guidance

The Quran highlights the role of divine guidance (Hidayah) in shaping human choices and actions. While humans have the free will to choose their path, Allah provides guidance to those who seek it. The Quran states, "And those who strive for Us – We will surely guide them to Our ways. And indeed, Allah is with the doers of good" (Quran 29:69). This verse emphasizes that sincere effort and striving are met with divine guidance, leading individuals towards righteousness.

Divine guidance operates through various means, including the revelation of the Quran, the teachings of the Prophet

Muhammad (PBUH), and the inner light of conscience. By aligning their will with divine guidance, believers can navigate the complexities of life, making choices that reflect their commitment to Allah's will.

The Interplay in Historical and Personal Contexts

The interplay of free will and divine will can be observed in both historical and personal contexts. The Quran recounts numerous stories of prophets and nations, illustrating how divine will shapes the course of history while allowing for human agency. The story of Prophet Moses (Musa) and Pharaoh is a prime example, where divine decree and human actions interact to fulfil Allah's greater plan.

On a personal level, the interplay is evident in the daily choices and decisions that individuals make. The Quran states, "Indeed, Allah will not change the condition of a people until they change what is in themselves" (Quran 13:11). This verse highlights the proactive role that humans must play in seeking personal and communal transformation, while recognizing that ultimate success and change are in Allah's hands.

The Eschatological Perspective

The ultimate resolution of the interplay between free will and divine will is found in the eschatological vision of the Quran. The Day of Judgment is depicted as a time when the true nature of every deed and intention will be revealed, and divine justice will be perfectly realized. The Quran states, "Then is one who was a believer like one who was defiantly disobedient? They are not equal. As for those who believed and did righteous deeds, for them will be the Gardens of Refuge, as accommodation for what they used to do. But as for those who defiantly disobeyed, their refuge is the Fire. Every time they wish to emerge from it, they will be returned to it while it is said to them, 'Taste the punishment of the Fire which you used to deny'" (Quran 32:18-20).

This eschatological perspective reinforces the significance of free will and moral accountability, while affirming that divine will ultimately prevails. It provides a comprehensive framework for understanding the consequences of human actions and the fulfilment of divine justice.

Conclusion: Embracing the Interplay of Free Will and Divine Will

The interplay of free will and divine will, as presented in the Quran, offers a profound and nuanced understanding of human existence. It emphasizes the balance between human agency and divine sovereignty, highlighting the moral and ethical responsibilities of individuals while affirming the ultimate control of Allah SWT.

As we continue our metaphysical odyssey, we are called to reflect on the deeper meanings of free will and divine will, recognizing their coexistence in shaping our lives and destinies. By aligning our intentions and actions with divine guidance, trusting in Allah's wisdom, and striving for righteousness, we can navigate the complexities of life with confidence and faith. This journey towards understanding the interplay of free will and divine will leads to intellectual enlightenment.

CHAPTER 7

The Signs of Allah in Nature

Introduction to Divine Signs

The natural world is replete with signs (ayat) that point to the existence, power, and wisdom of Allah SWT. These signs invite us to contemplate the intricate beauty and complexity of creation, prompting a deeper appreciation of the divine artistry that underlies the universe. The Quran frequently urges believers to observe and reflect upon the natural world, recognizing it as a manifestation of Allah's presence. This chapter explores the Quranic perspective on the signs of Allah in nature, examining their significance for spiritual growth, scientific inquiry, and ethical behaviour.

The Quranic Call to Contemplation

The Quran emphasizes the importance of contemplating the natural world as a means of recognizing Allah's signs. Verses such as, "Indeed, in the creation of the heavens and the earth and the alternation of the night and the day are signs for those of understanding" (Quran 3:190), encourage believers to reflect upon the wonders of creation. This contemplation is not merely an intellectual exercise; it is a spiritual practice that fosters a deeper connection with the Creator.

The Quranic call to contemplation is rooted in the belief that the natural world is a reflection of divine attributes. By observing the order, harmony, and beauty of creation, we gain insights into Allah's wisdom, power, and mercy. This process of reflection deepens our faith and enhances our understanding of the divine.

The Signs in the Heavens

The heavens, with their vastness and splendour, are among the most striking signs of Allah's creation. The Quran frequently references the celestial bodies as manifestations of divine power and precision. Verses such as, "And He it is who created the night and the day, and the sun and the moon; all [heavenly bodies] swim along, each in its rounded course" (Quran 21:33), highlight the orderly movement of celestial objects as signs of divine order.

The regularity and precision of celestial phenomena, such as the phases of the moon, the cycles of the sun, and the constellations of stars, reflect the disciplined nature of creation. These phenomena not only provide a sense of awe and wonder but also serve practical purposes, such as measuring time and guiding navigation. By contemplating the heavens, we are reminded of Allah's meticulous design and the vastness of His creation.

The Signs in the Earth

The Earth, with its diverse landscapes and ecosystems, is another profound manifestation of Allah's signs. The Quran invites us to observe the variety of life forms, the fertility of the soil, and the balance of natural cycles as evidence of divine wisdom. Verses such as, "And the earth – We spread it out and cast therein firmly set mountains and made grow therein [something] of every beautiful kind" (Quran 50:7), emphasize the beauty and diversity of terrestrial creation.

The interconnectedness of ecosystems, the cycles of growth and decay, and the provision of sustenance through plants and animals all point to a purposeful and benevolent Creator. By reflecting on the signs in the earth, we develop a greater appreciation for the sustenance and balance provided by Allah, fostering a sense of gratitude and stewardship.

The Signs in Water

Water is a fundamental element of life, and its role in creation is prominently highlighted in the Quran. Verses such as, "And We made from water every living thing. Then will they not believe?" (Quran 21:30), underscore the essential nature of water and its significance as a divine sign. The distribution of water through rivers, rain, and oceans, as well as its role in sustaining life, reflects Allah's mercy and provision.

The Quran also emphasizes the miraculous properties of water, such as its ability to sustain life, purify, and facilitate growth. By contemplating the signs in water, we recognize the interconnectedness of all life forms and the divine wisdom that sustains this delicate balance. This recognition fosters a sense of responsibility to preserve and protect this vital resource.

The Signs in the Plant Kingdom

The plant kingdom, with its diversity and complexity, is another profound manifestation of Allah's signs. The Quran frequently references plants, trees, and fruits as evidence of divine creativity and provision. Verses such as, "And it is He who sends down rain from the sky, and We produce thereby the growth of all things. We produce from it greenery from which We produce grains arranged in layers. And from the palm trees – of its emerging fruit are clusters hanging low. And [We produce] gardens of grapevines and olives and pomegranates, similar yet varied. Look at [each of] its fruit when it yields and [at] its ripening. Indeed in that are signs for a people who believe" (Quran 6:99), highlight the diversity and abundance of plant life as signs of Allah's provision.

The processes of germination, growth, and reproduction in plants reflect the intricate and purposeful design of creation. By contemplating these processes, we gain insights into the cycles of life and the sustaining power of Allah. This reflection fosters a sense of wonder and gratitude for the natural bounty provided by the Creator.

The Signs in the Animal Kingdom

The animal kingdom, with its vast array of species and behaviours, is another testament to Allah's creative power. The Quran invites us to observe the diversity and complexity of animal life as signs of divine wisdom. Verses such as, "And there is no creature on or within the earth or bird that flies with its wings except [that they are] communities like you. We have not neglected in the Register a thing. Then unto their Lord they will be gathered" (Quran

6:38), emphasize the interconnectedness of all living beings and their role within the divine order.

The behaviours and adaptations of animals, from the intricate social structures of bees to the migratory patterns of birds, reflect the wisdom and creativity of Allah. By contemplating the signs in the animal kingdom, we develop a deeper appreciation for the diversity and complexity of life, fostering a sense of humility and respect for all creatures.

The Integration of Scientific Inquiry and Spiritual Reflection

The Quranic perspective on the signs of Allah in nature encourages a harmonious integration of scientific inquiry and spiritual reflection. The pursuit of knowledge about the natural world is seen as a means of deepening one's faith and understanding of the Creator. Verses such as, "Do they not look into the realm of the heavens and the earth and everything that Allah has created?" (Quran 7:185), invite believers to explore and study the natural world as a way of recognizing divine signs.

Scientific discoveries about the intricacies of the natural world, from the genetic code to the vastness of the cosmos, provide opportunities for marvelling at the divine artistry. The Quran encourages believers to use their intellect and observation to uncover the hidden wonders of creation, thereby strengthening their faith and appreciation of Allah's wisdom.

The Ethical Implications of Recognizing Divine Signs

Recognizing the signs of Allah in nature has profound ethical implications. The Quran teaches that the natural world is a trust (amanah) from Allah, and humans are responsible for its stewardship. Verses such as, "It is He who has made you successors upon the earth and has raised some of you above others in degrees [of rank] that He may try you through what He has given you" (Quran 6:165), highlight the responsibility of humans to care for and protect the environment.

The recognition of divine signs in nature fosters a sense of respect and reverence for all creation. It encourages sustainable practices, conservation of resources, and ethical treatment of all living beings. By embracing the role of stewards, believers fulfil their responsibility to protect and preserve the natural world for future generations.

The Spiritual Benefits of Contemplating Divine Signs

Contemplating the signs of Allah in nature offers numerous spiritual benefits. It deepens one's sense of awe and wonder, enhances gratitude for the Creator's blessings, and strengthens the connection with Allah. This reflection fosters a sense of inner peace and contentment, as believers recognize the divine wisdom and mercy that permeate every aspect of creation.

The practice of observing and reflecting on nature also encourages mindfulness and presence, helping individuals to remain grounded in the present moment. By immersing oneself in the beauty and complexity of the natural world, believers can cultivate a deeper sense of spirituality and a more profound connection with the Creator.

Conclusion: Embracing the Signs of Allah in Nature

The signs of Allah in nature, as presented in the Quran, offer a rich and multifaceted understanding of the divine presence in the world. By contemplating the heavens, the earth, water, plants, and animals, believers are invited to recognize the intricate beauty and wisdom of Allah's creation. This recognition fosters a deeper sense of faith, gratitude, and responsibility.

As we continue our metaphysical odyssey, we are called to reflect on the signs of Allah in nature, integrating scientific inquiry with spiritual reflection. By embracing the ethical implications of recognizing divine signs and cultivating a sense of awe and wonder, we can enhance our spiritual growth and deepen our connection with the Creator. This journey towards understanding the signs of Allah in nature leads to intellectual enlightenment, spiritual fulfilment, and a greater appreciation of the divine artistry that underlies all existence.

CHAPTER 8

The Soul and Its Journey

Introduction to the Concept of the Soul

The concept of the soul is central to many philosophical, theological, and spiritual traditions. In the Islamic worldview, the soul (ruh) is a profound and mysterious entity that transcends the physical body, representing the essence of human identity and the connection to the divine. The Quran provides a comprehensive framework for understanding the nature, purpose, and journey of the soul, offering insights into its origin, life experiences, and ultimate destiny. This chapter delves deeply into the Quranic perspective on the soul, exploring its metaphysical dimensions, its journey through life and the hereafter, and its implications for human existence and spirituality.

The Origin and Nature of the Soul

The Quran asserts that the soul is a divine creation, breathed into the human body by Allah. This divine origin is emphasized in verses such as, "And when I have proportioned him and breathed into him of My [created] soul, then fall down to him in prostration" (Quran 15:29). This verse highlights the unique status of the human soul, which is directly linked to the divine breath, signifying a profound connection with Allah.

The nature of the soul is complex and multifaceted. It is described as a luminous entity that encompasses consciousness, intellect, and spiritual awareness. The soul is distinct from the physical body, yet intimately connected to it, serving as the animating force that brings life and vitality. The Quranic view of the soul emphasizes its immaterial and eternal nature, suggesting that it transcends the limitations of the physical world.

The Duality of Human Nature

The Quran presents a nuanced understanding of human nature, characterized by a duality between the physical and spiritual dimensions. This duality is reflected in verses such as, "We have certainly created man into hardship" (Quran 90:4), which alludes to the challenges and struggles inherent in the human condition. The physical body is subject to worldly desires and limitations, while the soul aspires to higher spiritual goals and a connection with the divine.

This duality creates a dynamic tension within the human experience, where the soul strives to overcome the influences of the ego (nafs) and align itself with divine guidance. The Quran emphasizes the importance of purifying the soul through acts of worship, ethical conduct, and self-discipline. Verses such as, "He has succeeded who purifies it, and he has failed who instils it [with corruption]" (Quran 91:9-10), underscore the significance of spiritual purification in achieving true success.

The Journey of the Soul in Life

The journey of the soul begins with its creation and entry into the physical body. This journey is marked by various stages of development, each presenting opportunities for growth, learning, and spiritual advancement. The Quran provides guidance on how to navigate this journey, emphasizing the importance of faith, righteous deeds, and adherence to divine commandments.

The soul's journey in life is characterized by continuous striving and self-improvement. The Quran states, "And that there is not for man except that [good] for which he strives and that his effort is going to be seen" (Quran 53:39-40). This verse highlights the principle of personal responsibility and the significance of intentional effort in shaping one's spiritual destiny.

The Role of Intellect and Free Will

The Quran acknowledges the vital role of intellect (aql) and free will (ikhtiyar) in the journey of the soul. Intellect is viewed as a divine gift that enables humans to discern truth, make ethical decisions, and seek knowledge. The Quran encourages the use of intellect to reflect upon the signs of Allah, engage in critical thinking, and pursue a deeper understanding of the divine.

Free will is equally significant, as it empowers individuals to make choices that shape their moral and spiritual development. The Quran emphasizes that humans are accountable for their actions, and their choices have profound implications for their soul's journey. Verses such as, "And say, 'The truth is from your Lord, so whoever wills – let him believe; and whoever wills – let him disbelieve'" (Quran 18:29), underscore the principle of free will and its centrality to human experience.

The Challenges and Trials of Life

The journey of the soul is replete with challenges and trials, which serve as tests of faith and opportunities for spiritual growth. The Quran teaches that trials are an integral part of the divine plan, designed to refine and strengthen the soul. Verses such as, "And We will surely test you with something of fear and hunger and a loss of wealth and lives and fruits, but give good tidings to the patient" (Quran 2:155), highlight the purpose and significance of trials in the human experience.

These challenges require the soul to exercise patience (sabr), perseverance, and trust in Allah's wisdom. By facing and overcoming trials, the soul develops resilience and spiritual maturity, drawing closer to the divine. The Quran provides numerous examples of prophets and righteous individuals who endured great hardships with unwavering faith, serving as role models for believers.

The Role of Worship and Spiritual Practices

Worship (ibadah) and spiritual practices play a central role in the journey of the soul. The Quran emphasizes the importance of regular acts of worship, such as prayer (salah), fasting (sawm), and charity (zakat), as means of purifying the soul and strengthening its connection with Allah. These practices are not merely ritualistic; they are profound spiritual disciplines that nurture the soul and foster a sense of divine presence.

The Quran states, "And I did not create the jinn and mankind except to worship Me" (Quran 51:56), underscoring the ultimate purpose of human existence as worship. Through worship, the soul transcends the distractions and temptations of the physical world, attaining a state of spiritual elevation and closeness to

Allah. Acts of worship also serve as reminders of the soul's true nature and its eternal destiny.

The Journey of the Soul After Death

The Quran provides a detailed and vivid portrayal of the soul's journey after death, encompassing the stages of the grave (barzakh), the Day of Judgment (Yawm al-Qiyamah), and the eternal abode in the hereafter (akhirah). This journey is marked by a transition from the temporal, physical world to the eternal, spiritual realm, where the soul's true nature is fully realized.

The stage of the grave is described as an intermediate realm where the soul awaits the Day of Judgment. The Quran states, "And behind them is a barrier until the Day they are resurrected" (Quran 23:100). This period is characterized by a state of awareness and anticipation, where the soul experiences the consequences of its earthly deeds.

The Day of Judgment is depicted as a momentous event when all souls are resurrected and held accountable for their actions. The Quran emphasizes the meticulous nature of divine justice, stating, "So whoever does an atom's weight of good will see it, and whoever does an atom's weight of evil will see it" (Quran 99:7-8). This day represents the culmination of the soul's journey, where it receives its final recompense based on its faith and deeds.

The eternal abode in the hereafter is described in vivid and contrasting terms, with Paradise (Jannah) representing the ultimate reward for the righteous and Hell (Jahannam) as the abode of punishment for the wicked. The Quran provides detailed descriptions of the joys and blessings of Paradise, as well as the torments and sufferings of Hell, emphasizing the eternal nature of these abodes.

The Eternal Nature of the Soul

The Quran affirms the eternal nature of the soul, emphasizing that its journey does not end with physical death. The soul's experiences in the hereafter are characterized by a state of permanence and continuity, reflecting its true essence. Verses such as, "Every soul will taste death. Then to Us will you be returned" (Quran 29:57), highlight the transient nature of physical life and the enduring reality of the soul.

The eternal nature of the soul underscores the significance of the choices and actions made in this life. The Quran teaches that the soul's ultimate destiny is shaped by its faith, deeds, and adherence to divine guidance. This understanding fosters a sense of urgency and purpose in the believer's life, encouraging them to strive for righteousness and spiritual excellence.

The Spiritual Significance of the Soul's Journey

The journey of the soul, as presented in the Quran, offers profound spiritual insights and guidance for human existence. It emphasizes the importance of self-awareness, ethical conduct, and spiritual discipline in navigating the complexities of life. By understanding the nature and purpose of the soul, believers can cultivate a deeper connection with Allah and a more meaningful approach to life.

The journey of the soul also fosters a sense of humility and gratitude, as individuals recognize their dependence on Allah's mercy and guidance. It encourages a holistic approach to spirituality, integrating worship, ethical behaviour, and self-reflection as means of purifying and elevating the soul.

Conclusion: Embracing the Journey of the Soul

The Quranic perspective on the soul and its journey offers a rich and multifaceted understanding of human existence. By contemplating the divine origin, nature, and destiny of the soul, believers are invited to recognize the profound connection between their spiritual essence and the Creator. This recognition fosters a deeper sense of faith, purpose, and responsibility.

As we continue our metaphysical odyssey, we are called to reflect on the journey of the soul, embracing the principles of worship, ethical conduct, and spiritual discipline. By aligning our lives with divine guidance and striving for spiritual purification, we can navigate the challenges of life with resilience and grace. This journey towards understanding the soul and its ultimate destiny leads to intellectual enlightenment, spiritual fulfilment, and a profound connection with the Creator.

CHAPTER 9

The Metaphysics of Morality

Introduction to the Metaphysics of Morality

Morality is a fundamental aspect of human existence, guiding our actions, shaping our character, and influencing our relationships. The concept of morality transcends cultural and temporal boundaries, reflecting universal principles of right and wrong, justice and injustice, virtue and vice. In the Islamic worldview, morality is deeply rooted in the metaphysical framework provided by the Quran, which offers a comprehensive guide to ethical conduct based on divine revelation. This chapter delves into the metaphysics of morality from a Quranic perspective, exploring its foundations, principles, and implications for personal and societal well-being.

The Divine Origin of Morality

The Quran asserts that morality is derived from the divine will of Allah SWT, who is the ultimate source of all ethical principles. This divine origin is emphasized in verses such as, "Indeed, Allah commands justice, good conduct, and giving to relatives and forbids immorality, bad conduct, and oppression. He admonishes you that perhaps you will be reminded" (Quran 16:90). This verse highlights that ethical values are not arbitrary but are rooted in the divine attributes of justice, mercy, and wisdom.

The Quranic view of morality is intrinsically linked to the concept of Tawhid, the oneness of Allah. Tawhid implies that all aspects of life, including moral conduct, are governed by the recognition of Allah's sovereignty and authority. By adhering to the ethical guidelines provided by Allah, believers align themselves with the divine order and fulfil their purpose as His servants.

The Nature of Good and Evil

The Quran provides a clear delineation between good (ma'ruf) and evil (munkar), emphasizing that these concepts are objective and absolute. Good is defined by actions that align with divine commands and promote justice, compassion, and righteousness, while evil encompasses actions that contravene these principles and lead to harm, injustice, and corruption.

The Quran states, "Say, 'Not equal are the evil and the good, although the abundance of evil might impress you. So fear Allah, O you of understanding, that you may be successful'" (Quran 5:100). This verse underscores the distinction between good and evil, urging believers to use their understanding and fear of Allah to make ethical choices. The metaphysical nature of good and evil reflects the intrinsic order of creation, where moral principles are embedded in the fabric of reality.

The Role of Conscience and Intellect

Conscience (dhamir) and intellect (aql) play crucial roles in the Quranic framework of morality. The conscience is viewed as an inner sense of right and wrong, a moral compass that guides individuals in their ethical decision-making. The Quran states, "And [by] the soul and He who proportioned it and inspired it with discernment of its wickedness and its righteousness" (Quran 91:7-8). This verse highlights that Allah has endowed the soul with an innate ability to discern moral truths.

Intellect, on the other hand, is seen as a divine gift that enables humans to reflect, reason, and understand ethical principles. The Quran encourages the use of intellect to contemplate moral issues, recognize divine signs, and seek knowledge. Verses such as, "Indeed, in the creation of the heavens and the earth and the alternation of the night and the day are signs for those of understanding" (Quran 3:190), emphasize the importance of intellectual engagement in moral and spiritual growth.

The Principles of Islamic Morality

Islamic morality is built upon several foundational principles that guide ethical conduct. These principles include justice (adl), compassion (rahmah), truthfulness (sidq), and responsibility (amanah). Each of these principles is rooted in the divine attributes of Allah and is reflected in the Quranic teachings.

Justice is a central principle of Islamic morality, reflecting Allah's attribute of being the Just (Al-Adl). The Quran states, "O you who have believed, be persistently standing firm in justice, witnesses for Allah, even if it be against yourselves or parents and relatives" (Quran 4:135). This verse underscores the importance of upholding justice in all circumstances, even when it is difficult or against one's interests.

Compassion is another key principle, reflecting Allah's attribute of being the Most Merciful (Ar-Rahman). The Quran emphasizes the importance of showing kindness and mercy to others, stating, "And We have not sent you, [O Muhammad], except as a mercy to the worlds" (Quran 21:107). This principle encourages believers to embody compassion in their interactions, promoting social harmony and care for the vulnerable.

Truthfulness is a fundamental aspect of Islamic morality, reflecting Allah's attribute of being the Truth (Al-Haqq). The Quran commands believers to speak the truth and act with integrity, stating, "O you who have believed, fear Allah and speak words of appropriate justice" (Quran 33:70). Truthfulness fosters trust and transparency, essential for healthy relationships and communities.

Responsibility is also a core principle, reflecting the concept of amanah (trust). The Quran teaches that humans are stewards of the earth and are responsible for their actions and their impact on others. Verses such as, "Indeed, We offered the Trust to the heavens and the earth and the mountains, and they declined to bear it and feared it; but man [undertook to] bear it. Indeed, he was unjust and ignorant" (Quran 33:72), highlight the gravity of this responsibility and the need for conscientious stewardship.

The Integration of Worship and Morality

In the Quranic worldview, worship (ibadah) and morality are inseparable, each reinforcing the other. Acts of worship, such as prayer, fasting, and charity, are not merely ritualistic practices but are deeply connected to ethical conduct. The Quran states, "Indeed, prayer prohibits immorality and wrongdoing, and the remembrance of Allah is greater. And Allah knows that which you do" (Quran 29:45). This verse underscores that genuine worship cultivates moral integrity and deters unethical behaviour.

Fasting during the month of Ramadan is another example of the integration of worship and morality. The Quran emphasizes that fasting is intended to foster self-discipline, empathy, and righteousness, stating, "O you who have believed, decreed upon you is fasting as it was decreed upon those before you that you may become righteous" (Quran 2:183). By abstaining from physical needs, believers develop greater awareness of their moral and spiritual responsibilities.

Charity (zakat) is a further manifestation of this integration, as it directly addresses social justice and the welfare of the needy. The Quran commands, "Take, [O Muhammad], from their wealth a charity by which you purify them and cause them increase, and invoke [Allah's blessings] upon them. Indeed, your invocations are reassurance for them. And Allah is Hearing and Knowing" (Quran 9:103). By giving to those in need, believers purify their wealth and cultivate compassion and social responsibility.

The Ethical Dimensions of Social Justice

Social justice is a central theme in the Quranic framework of morality, reflecting the divine attributes of justice and compassion. The Quran calls for the establishment of a just society where the rights of all individuals are upheld, and the vulnerable are protected. Verses such as, "O you who have believed, be persistently standing firm for Allah, witnesses in justice, and do not let the hatred of a people prevent you from being just. Be just; that is nearer to righteousness. And fear Allah; indeed, Allah is Acquainted with what you do" (Quran 5:8), highlight the importance of impartial justice and ethical conduct.

The Quran also emphasizes the need to address economic inequality and provide for those in need. Verses such as, "And in their wealth was a right for the petitioner and the deprived" (Quran 51:19), underscore the moral obligation to share resources and support the less fortunate. This principle of economic justice promotes social cohesion and reduces disparities, fostering a more equitable society.

The Role of Prophets as Moral Exemplars

The prophets, as messengers of Allah, serve as moral exemplars who embody the ethical principles outlined in the Quran. Their lives and teachings provide practical guidance on how to navigate moral challenges and live righteously. The Quran states, "There has certainly been for you in the Messenger of Allah an excellent pattern for anyone whose hope is in Allah and the Last Day and [who] remembers Allah often" (Quran 33:21). This verse highlights the Prophet Muhammad (PBUH) as a role model for ethical conduct and spiritual devotion.

The stories of other prophets, such as Prophet Ibrahim (Abraham), Prophet Musa (Moses), and Prophet Isa (Jesus), also offer valuable lessons in morality. Their examples of faith, perseverance, and commitment to justice serve as timeless guides for believers. By studying their lives, believers can gain insights into the practical application of Quranic ethics and the importance of moral integrity.

The Eschatological Dimension of Morality

The Quranic perspective on morality is intrinsically linked to the eschatological vision of the Day of Judgment. The belief in an afterlife and divine accountability provides a powerful incentive for ethical conduct. The Quran emphasizes that every action, no matter how small, will be accounted for and judged by Allah. Verses such as, "So whoever does an atom's weight of good will see it, and whoever does an atom's weight of evil will see it" (Quran 99:7-8), underscore the meticulous nature of divine justice.

The eschatological dimension of morality reinforces the significance of living a righteous life, knowing that ultimate justice will be realized in the hereafter. This belief fosters a sense of moral responsibility and encourages believers to strive for ethical excellence in all aspects of their lives.

CHAPTER 10

The Unseen World

Introduction to the Unseen World

The concept of the unseen world (al-ghayb) is a profound and central theme in Islamic theology, encompassing the metaphysical realities that lie beyond human perception. The Quran repeatedly emphasizes the significance of believing in the unseen as a fundamental aspect of faith. This chapter delves into the intricate dimensions of the unseen world, exploring its various components, such as angels, jinn, and other metaphysical entities, and examining their roles and implications for human life and spirituality.

The Quranic Emphasis on Belief in the Unseen

Belief in the unseen is a cornerstone of the Islamic faith, as highlighted in the Quran: "This is the Book about which there is no doubt, a guidance for those conscious of Allah –who believe in the unseen, establish prayer, and spend out of what We have provided for them" (Quran 2:2-3). This verse underscores that faith in the unseen is integral to recognizing and accepting divine guidance.

The unseen world encompasses entities and realms that are not accessible through sensory perception or empirical observation. This belief challenges the materialistic worldview and invites believers to acknowledge a reality that transcends the physical world. It fosters a deeper connection with the divine, encouraging a holistic understanding of existence that includes both the seen and the unseen.

The Nature and Role of Angels

Angels (mala'ika) are among the most significant entities in the unseen world, serving as messengers and agents of Allah's will. The Quran provides detailed descriptions of the nature and functions of angels, emphasizing their obedience, purity, and devotion to Allah. Verses such as, "They exalt [Him] night and day [and] do not slacken" (Quran 21:20), highlight the ceaseless worship and servitude of angels.

Angels play various roles, including conveying divine revelations, recording human deeds, and executing Allah's commands. The archangel Jibril (Gabriel) is particularly prominent, as he was entrusted with delivering the Quran to Prophet Muhammad (PBUH). The Quran states, "Say, 'Whoever is an enemy to Gabriel – it is [none but] he who has brought it [i.e., the Quran] down upon your heart, [O Muhammad], by permission of Allah, confirming that which was before it and as guidance and good tidings for the believers'" (Quran 2:97).

The belief in angels reinforces the notion of divine oversight and guidance, assuring believers that they are never alone and that their actions are being observed and recorded. This awareness fosters a sense of accountability and encourages ethical conduct.

The Existence and Nature of Jinn

Jinn are another significant component of the unseen world, possessing unique characteristics and abilities distinct from humans and angels. The Quran describes the creation of jinn from smokeless fire: "And He created the jinn from a smokeless flame of fire" (Quran 55:15). Jinn, like humans, possess free will and are capable of choosing between good and evil.

The Quran acknowledges the dual nature of jinn, with some being righteous and others rebellious. The most notorious jinn is Iblis (Satan), who defied Allah's command to bow to Adam and was subsequently cast out of paradise. The Quran recounts this event, stating, "And [mention] when We said to the angels, 'Prostrate to Adam,' and they prostrated, except for Iblis. He was of the jinn and departed from the command of his Lord" (Quran 18:50).

The existence of jinn underscores the diversity of creation and the presence of metaphysical beings that influence the human world. The Quran advises believers to seek protection from the harmful influences of malevolent jinn through prayer and remembrance of Allah: "And say, 'My Lord, I seek refuge in You from the incitements of the devils, and I seek refuge in You, my Lord, lest they be present with me'" (Quran 23:97-98).

The Concept of Barzakh

Barzakh, an intermediate realm between life and the hereafter, is a critical aspect of the unseen world. It is described as a barrier or partition that separates the living from the dead, where souls reside until the Day of Judgment. The Quran states, "And behind them is a barrier until the Day they are resurrected" (Quran 23:100).

Barzakh represents a state of waiting and transition, where souls experience the consequences of their earthly deeds. The righteous souls find peace and comfort, while the wicked face suffering and remorse. This intermediate state serves as a reminder of the transient nature of life and the inevitability of divine judgment.

The concept of Barzakh emphasizes the continuity of existence beyond physical death and the importance of preparing for the hereafter. It encourages believers to live righteously and seek forgiveness, knowing that their actions will have lasting implications beyond this life.

The Day of Judgment and the Hereafter

The Quran provides a vivid and detailed depiction of the Day of Judgment (Yawm al-Qiyamah) and the hereafter (Akhirah), emphasizing their significance in the unseen world. The Day of Judgment is described as a momentous event when all souls will be resurrected, and their deeds will be weighed and judged by Allah. The Quran states, "The Day when mankind will stand before the Lord of the worlds?" (Quran 83:6).

On this day, every individual will be held accountable for their actions, and ultimate justice will be realized. The Quran highlights the meticulous nature of this judgment, stating, "So whoever does an atom's weight of good will see it, and whoever does an atom's weight of evil will see it" (Quran 99:7-8). This eschatological vision underscores the moral and ethical dimensions of human existence, reinforcing the significance of righteous conduct.

The hereafter is depicted in vivid and contrasting terms, with Paradise (Jannah) representing the ultimate reward for the righteous and Hell (Jahannam) as the abode of punishment for the wicked. The Quran provides detailed descriptions of the joys and blessings of Paradise: "And give good tidings to those who believe and do righteous deeds that they will have gardens [in Paradise] beneath which rivers flow. Whenever they are provided with a provision of fruit therefrom, they will say, 'This is what we were provided with before.' And it is given to them in likeness. And they will have therein purified spouses, and they will abide therein eternally" (Quran 2:25).

Conversely, the torments of Hell are described with stark imagery, emphasizing the consequences of rejecting faith and indulging in evil deeds: "But those who disbelieved and denied Our signs – those are the companions of Hellfire" (Quran 5:10). These descriptions serve as powerful reminders of the ultimate realities of the unseen world and the eternal outcomes of human choices.

The Role of Faith and Trust in the Unseen

Belief in the unseen requires faith (iman) and trust (tawakkul) in Allah's wisdom and justice. The Quran emphasizes that true faith involves accepting the realities of the unseen, even when they are beyond human comprehension. Verses such as, "Alif, Lam, Meem. This is the Book about which there is no doubt, a guidance for those conscious of Allah – who believe in the unseen, establish prayer, and spend out of what We have provided for them" (Quran 2:1-3), highlight the integral connection between faith and belief in the unseen.

Trusting in the unseen fosters a sense of peace and reliance on Allah, knowing that He is aware of all things and controls the outcomes. The Quran encourages believers to place their trust in Allah, stating, "And whoever relies upon Allah – then He is sufficient for him. Indeed, Allah will accomplish His purpose. Allah has already set for everything a [decreed] extent" (Quran 65:3). This trust empowers believers to navigate the uncertainties of life with confidence and resilience, assured of Allah's protection and guidance.

The Spiritual Benefits of Believing in the Unseen

Belief in the unseen offers numerous spiritual benefits, enhancing one's faith, humility, and sense of purpose. It fosters a deeper connection with Allah and a greater appreciation of His omnipotence and omniscience. By acknowledging the realities of the unseen world, believers cultivate a sense of awe and reverence for the divine, strengthening their commitment to worship and righteous living.

This belief also encourages mindfulness and self-awareness, as individuals recognize that their actions are observed and recorded by unseen beings. The awareness of divine oversight and accountability motivates ethical conduct and the pursuit of spiritual excellence. It also provides comfort and hope, knowing that Allah's justice will ultimately prevail and that the trials of this world are temporary.

The Ethical and Moral Implications

Belief in the unseen world has profound ethical and moral implications. It reinforces the significance of living a righteous life, guided by the principles of justice, compassion, and integrity. The awareness of divine accountability encourages individuals to act with sincerity and humility, striving to align their actions with divine commands.

This belief also fosters a sense of responsibility towards others, recognizing that ethical conduct extends beyond personal piety to encompass social justice and care for the vulnerable. The Quranic teachings on the unseen world emphasize the importance of upholding justice, supporting the needy, and promoting the common good, reflecting the holistic nature of Islamic ethics.

Conclusion: Embracing the Unseen World

The concept of the unseen world, as presented in the Quran, offers a rich and multifaceted understanding of existence. By contemplating the realities of angels, jinn, Barzakh, and the hereafter, believers are invited to expand their perception of reality and deepen their faith in Allah's wisdom and justice. This belief fosters a holistic approach to life.

CHAPTER 11

The Concept of Divine Mercy

Introduction to Divine Mercy

Divine mercy is a central theme in the Islamic faith, reflecting the infinite compassion and benevolence of Allah SWT. The Quran frequently emphasizes Allah's mercy, highlighting it as a fundamental attribute that permeates every aspect of creation and governance. This chapter delves into the multifaceted nature of divine mercy, exploring its theological foundations, its manifestations in the natural and moral orders, and its profound implications for human life and spirituality.

The Theological Foundations of Divine Mercy

The Quran opens with a declaration of Allah's mercy: "In the name of Allah, the Most Compassionate, the Most Merciful" (Quran 1:1). This phrase, known as the Basmala, is recited by Muslims at the beginning of various acts and underscores the centrality of mercy in the Islamic worldview. The attributes of compassion (Ar-Rahman) and mercy (Ar-Rahim) are repeatedly invoked, emphasizing that Allah's mercy is both boundless and encompassing.

The Quran asserts that divine mercy is an essential aspect of Allah's nature, reflecting His desire to guide, forgive, and nurture His creation. Verses such as, "And My mercy encompasses all things" (Quran 7:156), highlight the all-encompassing nature of Allah's mercy, suggesting that it extends to every aspect of existence. This theological foundation establishes a framework for understanding the profound and pervasive influence of divine mercy in the world.

Manifestations of Divine Mercy in Creation

The natural world is a testament to Allah's mercy, with countless signs that reflect His benevolence and care for creation. The Quran invites believers to contemplate these signs, recognizing them as manifestations of divine mercy. Verses such as, "And He has subjected to you whatever is in the heavens and whatever is on the earth – all from Him. Indeed, in that are signs for a people who give thought" (Quran 45:13), emphasize the provision and sustenance provided by Allah.

The cycles of nature, the abundance of resources, and the intricate balance of ecosystems all point to a compassionate Creator who nurtures and sustains life. The Quran states, "It is He who sends down rain from the sky; from it is drink and from it is foliage in which you pasture [animals]. He causes to grow for you thereby the crops, the olives, the palm trees, the grapevines, and from all the fruits. Indeed in that is a sign for a people who give thought" (Quran 16:10-11). This verse highlights the nurturing aspect of divine mercy, which ensures the flourishing of all living beings.

Divine Mercy in Human Life

Divine mercy is profoundly reflected in the human experience, encompassing guidance, forgiveness, and compassion. The Quran describes the revelation of guidance as an act of mercy, providing humanity with a clear path to righteousness and salvation. Verses such as, "And We have not sent you, [O Muhammad], except as a mercy to the worlds" (Quran 21:107), underscore the merciful nature of prophetic guidance.

Forgiveness is another critical manifestation of divine mercy in human life. The Quran emphasizes that Allah is always willing to forgive those who turn to Him in repentance. Verses such as, "Say, 'O My servants who have transgressed against themselves [by sinning], do not despair of the mercy of Allah. Indeed, Allah forgives all sins. Indeed, it is He who is the Forgiving, the Merciful'" (Quran 39:53), highlight the boundless nature of divine forgiveness, encouraging believers to seek repentance and reform.

Compassion is also a key aspect of divine mercy, reflected in the ethical and social teachings of Islam. The Quran instructs believers to emulate Allah's compassion by showing kindness and care to others, particularly the vulnerable and disadvantaged. Verses such as, "And lower to them the wing of humility out of mercy and say, 'My Lord, have mercy upon them as they brought me up [when I was] small'" (Quran 17:24), emphasize the importance of compassion in familial and social relationships.

The Balance Between Justice and Mercy

The Quran presents a balanced view of divine justice and mercy, emphasizing that while Allah is just, His mercy often overrides

His wrath. This balance is reflected in the Quranic descriptions of divine judgment, where mercy and forgiveness are offered to those who sincerely repent and seek Allah's guidance. Verses such as, "And your Lord is the Forgiving, Full of Mercy. If He were to impose blame upon them for what they earned, He would have hastened for them the punishment. But for them is an appointment from which they will never find an escape" (Quran 18:58), highlight the interplay between justice and mercy.

The balance between justice and mercy ensures that divine governance is both fair and compassionate. It provides a framework for understanding how Allah's mercy operates within the context of His overall plan for creation. This balance is particularly evident in the concept of divine forgiveness, where repentance and sincere efforts to reform are met with mercy and grace.

The Role of Mercy in Spiritual Growth

Divine mercy plays a pivotal role in the spiritual growth and development of believers. It serves as a source of hope and motivation, encouraging individuals to strive for righteousness and seek closeness to Allah. The Quran teaches that Allah's mercy is always accessible, providing a foundation for spiritual resilience and perseverance. Verses such as, "And My mercy encompasses all things. So I will decree it [especially] for those who fear Me and give zakah and those who believe in Our verses" (Quran 7:156), highlight the inclusive nature of divine mercy and its availability to those who seek it.

The awareness of divine mercy fosters a sense of gratitude and humility, as believers recognize their dependence on Allah's compassion and forgiveness. This awareness encourages a deeper commitment to worship, ethical conduct, and self-discipline. By aligning their actions with the principles of mercy, believers can cultivate a more compassionate and spiritually enriched life.

The Ethical Implications of Divine Mercy

Belief in divine mercy has profound ethical implications, shaping how individuals interact with others and approach their responsibilities. The Quran encourages believers to embody the principles of mercy in their daily lives, promoting compassion, forgiveness, and kindness. Verses such as, "And the servants of the Most Merciful are those who walk upon the earth easily, and when the ignorant address them [harshly], they say [words of] peace" (Quran 25:63), highlight the importance of demonstrating mercy in interactions with others.

The ethical implications of divine mercy extend to social justice and the treatment of the vulnerable. The Quran instructs believers to support the needy, protect the oppressed, and promote equity and fairness. Verses such as, "And they give food in spite of love for it to the needy, the orphan, and the captive, [Saying], 'We feed you only for the countenance of Allah. We wish not from you reward or gratitude'" (Quran 76:8-9), emphasize the selfless nature of compassionate acts and their significance in the eyes of Allah.

The Eschatological Perspective of Divine Mercy

The Quran presents an eschatological vision where divine mercy plays a crucial role in the ultimate fate of individuals. The Day of

Judgment is depicted as a time when Allah's mercy will be fully manifested, offering hope and salvation to the righteous. Verses such as, "And your Lord will give you, and you will be satisfied" (Quran 93:5), highlight the promise of divine reward and the fulfilment of Allah's mercy.

In the hereafter, the ultimate expression of divine mercy is the admission of the righteous into Paradise (Jannah). The Quran describes Paradise as a place of eternal bliss, prepared for those who have lived righteously and sought Allah's mercy. Verses such as, "But those who feared their Lord will be driven to Paradise in groups until, when they reach it while its gates have been opened and its keepers say, 'Peace be upon you; you have become pure; so enter it to abide eternally therein'" (Quran 39:73), depict the welcoming of the righteous into Paradise as an act of divine mercy.

The Spiritual Benefits of Embracing Divine Mercy

Embracing the concept of divine mercy offers numerous spiritual benefits, enhancing one's faith, resilience, and sense of purpose. It fosters a deep sense of peace and security, knowing that Allah's mercy is always available and that forgiveness is attainable. This understanding encourages believers to continually seek repentance and strive for spiritual improvement.

The awareness of divine mercy also promotes a positive and compassionate outlook on life, encouraging individuals to approach challenges with hope and trust in Allah's wisdom. By embodying the principles of mercy, believers can cultivate stronger relationships, contribute to a more just and compassionate society, and achieve a greater sense of spiritual fulfilment.

Conclusion: Embracing Divine Mercy

The concept of divine mercy, as presented in the Quran, offers a profound and comprehensive understanding of Allah's compassion and benevolence. By contemplating the theological foundations, manifestations in creation, and ethical implications of divine mercy, believers are invited to recognize its pervasive influence in their lives. This recognition fosters a deeper connection with Allah, encouraging a more compassionate and spiritually enriched approach to life.

As we continue our metaphysical odyssey, we are called to reflect on the significance of divine mercy, integrating its principles into our daily actions and interactions. By embracing the balance between justice and mercy, seeking spiritual growth, and promoting ethical conduct, we can navigate the complexities of life with confidence and grace. This journey towards understanding and embodying divine mercy leads to intellectual enlightenment, spiritual fulfilment, and a profound connection with the Creator.

CHAPTER 12

The Ultimate Reality

Introduction to Ultimate Reality

The quest to understand ultimate reality is one of humanity's most profound and enduring pursuits. This exploration seeks to uncover the fundamental nature of existence, the underlying principles that govern the universe, and the relationship between the Creator and creation. In the Islamic worldview, the concept of ultimate reality is deeply intertwined with the notion of Allah SWT as the singular, absolute, and transcendent source of all that exists. This chapter delves into the Quranic perspective on ultimate reality, examining its theological, metaphysical, and existential dimensions, and exploring its implications for human understanding and spiritual growth.

The Concept of Tawhid

The cornerstone of Islamic theology is the concept of Tawhid, the oneness and unity of Allah. Tawhid asserts that Allah is the singular, absolute reality, the source and sustainer of all creation. This foundational belief is encapsulated in the declaration of faith: "La ilaha illallah" (There is no god but Allah). The Quran emphasizes the uniqueness and incomparability of Allah, stating,

"Say, 'He is Allah, [who is] One, Allah, the Eternal Refuge. He neither begets nor is born, nor is there to Him any equivalent'" (Quran 112:1-4).

Tawhid transcends the mere acknowledgment of monotheism; it encompasses the understanding that Allah's essence, attributes, and actions are unified and indivisible. This concept forms the basis for comprehending ultimate reality, as it posits that all phenomena in the universe are manifestations of Allah's will and attributes. The recognition of Tawhid invites believers to see beyond the multiplicity of the physical world and perceive the underlying unity that connects all things.

The Attributes of Allah

Understanding ultimate reality involves contemplating the attributes (sifat) of Allah as described in the Quran. These attributes provide insights into the nature of the divine and the principles that govern creation. Some of the key attributes include:

1. Al-Wahid (The One): Allah's singularity and uniqueness, emphasizing that He has no partners or equals.
2. Al-Hayy (The Ever-Living): Allah's eternal existence, underscoring that He is not subject to birth, death, or decay.
3. Al-Qayyum (The Sustainer): Allah's role as the sustainer and maintainer of all creation, ensuring the continuous existence and order of the universe.
4. Al-Alim (The All-Knowing): Allah's omniscience, indicating that He possesses complete and perfect knowledge of all things, past, present, and future.

5. Al-Qadir (The All-Powerful): Allah's omnipotence, affirming that He has the power to accomplish anything and everything according to His will.
6. Al-Adl (The Just): Allah's perfect justice, ensuring that all actions and events are governed by divine wisdom and fairness.
7. Ar-Rahman (The Most Compassionate) and Ar-Rahim (The Most Merciful): Allah's boundless compassion and mercy, which permeate every aspect of creation.

These attributes collectively define the ultimate reality, portraying a divine essence that is both transcendent and immanent, beyond human comprehension yet intimately involved in the workings of the universe.

The Metaphysical Framework of Creation

The Quran presents a metaphysical framework that describes the relationship between Allah and creation. This framework emphasizes that the physical world is not an independent reality but a manifestation of Allah's creative will. The Quran states, "Allah is the Creator of all things, and He is, over all things, Disposer of affairs" (Quran 39:62). This verse underscores that every aspect of existence is contingent upon Allah's will and power.

The concept of creation ex nihilo (creation from nothing) further highlights Allah's absolute sovereignty over the universe. The Quran affirms that Allah brought the cosmos into being through a simple command, "Be," and it was. "His command is only when He intends a thing that He says to it, 'Be,' and it is" (Quran 36:82). This act of creation underscores the ultimate reality that Allah is the origin and sustainer of all that exists.

The Quranic narrative also describes the purpose and order inherent in creation. Verses such as, "And We did not create the heaven and earth and everything between them in play. We did not create them except in truth, but most of them do not know" (Quran 44:38-39), emphasize that creation is purposeful and reflects divine wisdom. This purposeful creation invites believers to seek understanding and alignment with the divine order, recognizing the ultimate reality that governs all existence.

The Human Experience of Ultimate Reality

The Quran teaches that humans, as conscious beings, are uniquely positioned to contemplate and connect with ultimate reality. This connection is facilitated through intellect, reflection, and spiritual practices. The Quran encourages believers to use their intellect to ponder the signs of Allah in the universe: "Indeed, in the creation of the heavens and the earth and the alternation of the night and the day are signs for those of understanding" (Quran 3:190).

Reflection (tafakkur) and contemplation (tadabbur) are essential practices for perceiving ultimate reality. By contemplating the natural world, human experiences, and the divine revelation, believers can gain insights into the underlying principles that govern existence. This process of reflection leads to a deeper awareness of Allah's presence and a greater appreciation of the unity and harmony that characterize ultimate reality.

Spiritual practices, such as prayer (salah), fasting (sawm), and remembrance (dhikr), also play a crucial role in connecting with ultimate reality. These practices cultivate mindfulness, humility, and devotion, fostering a sense of closeness to Allah. The Quran emphasizes that through sincere worship and devotion, believers can attain a state of spiritual enlightenment and alignment with the divine will: "And establish prayer for My remembrance" (Quran 20:14).

The Relationship Between Free Will and Divine Will

The interplay between free will (ikhtiyar) and divine will (mashi'a) is a critical aspect of understanding ultimate reality. The Quran teaches that while Allah's will encompasses all things, humans are endowed with free will to make choices and are held accountable for their actions. This dynamic relationship is encapsulated in the verse, "And say, 'The truth is from your Lord, so whoever wills – let him believe; and whoever wills – let him disbelieve'" (Quran 18:29).

This balance between free will and divine will underscores the complexity and depth of ultimate reality. It affirms that human actions are meaningful and consequential, while also acknowledging that Allah's knowledge and power are absolute. The recognition of this interplay invites believers to exercise their free will responsibly, striving to align their choices with divine guidance and seeking Allah's pleasure.

The Role of Revelation in Understanding Ultimate Reality

The Quran, as the final revelation, provides a comprehensive guide to understanding ultimate reality. It offers a detailed account of the nature of Allah, the purpose of creation, and the principles that govern existence. The Quranic revelation serves as a source of knowledge, wisdom, and guidance, illuminating the path to spiritual enlightenment and closeness to Allah.

The Quran emphasizes that divine revelation is a mercy and a gift to humanity, providing clarity and insight into the mysteries of existence. Verses such as, "Indeed, this Quran guides to that which is most suitable and gives good tidings to the believers who do righteous deeds that they will have a great reward" (Quran 17:9), highlight the transformative power of the Quran in guiding believers towards a deeper understanding of ultimate reality.

The prophetic tradition (Sunnah) also plays a vital role in elucidating the teachings of the Quran and offering practical guidance on how to live in accordance with ultimate reality. The Prophet Muhammad (PBUH) serves as the exemplar of a life fully aligned with divine will, providing a model for believers to emulate in their pursuit of spiritual excellence.

The Eschatological Dimension of Ultimate Reality

The Quranic eschatology presents a vision of ultimate reality that extends beyond the temporal world to encompass the hereafter (akhirah). The belief in an afterlife, where souls are judged and recompensed based on their earthly deeds, is a fundamental aspect of understanding ultimate reality. The Quran describes the Day of Judgment (Yawm al-Qiyamah) as a momentous event when the true nature of existence is fully revealed, and divine justice is realized.

Verses such as, "The Day when they will come out of the graves quickly as if they were, toward an erected idol, hastening. Their eyes humbled, humiliation will cover them. That is the Day which they had been promised" (Quran 70:43-44), depict the transformative and revelatory nature of the Day of Judgment. This eschatological perspective reinforces the significance of living a righteous life, guided by the principles of Tawhid and divine guidance.

The ultimate reality of the hereafter is characterized by the eternal abodes of Paradise (Jannah) and Hell (Jahannam), where individuals experience the consequences of their earthly actions. The Quran provides vivid descriptions of these abodes, emphasizing the rewards and punishments that await the righteous and the wicked. Verses such as, "But those who believed and did righteous deeds will have gardens beneath which rivers flow. That is the great attainment" (Quran 85:11), highlight the ultimate fulfilment of divine promise and justice.

The Spiritual Implications of Ultimate Reality

Understanding ultimate reality has profound spiritual implications for believers. It fosters a sense of humility, gratitude, and awe, as individuals recognize their place within the divine order and their dependence on Allah's mercy and guidance. This understanding encourages a deeper commitment to worship, ethical conduct, and spiritual growth, as believers strive to align their lives with the principles of Tawhid.

CHAPTER 13

The Role of Prophethood

Introduction to Prophethood

Prophethood is a cornerstone of Islamic theology, representing the communication between Allah SWT and humanity. Prophets serve as messengers, guiding people toward a path of righteousness, ethical conduct, and spiritual awareness. The concept of prophethood underscores the importance of divine guidance in understanding and living according to the principles of ultimate reality. This chapter explores the Quranic perspective on the role of prophethood, examining its theological foundations, the characteristics and functions of prophets, and the implications for human life and spirituality.

The Theological Foundations of Prophethood

The Quran emphasizes the necessity of prophethood as a means of conveying divine guidance to humanity. Prophets are chosen individuals endowed with the responsibility of delivering Allah's messages, calling people to worship Him alone, and providing practical and moral guidance. The Quran states, "We have sent among you a Messenger of your own, reciting to you Our verses and purifying you and teaching you the Book and wisdom and teaching you that which you did not know" (Quran 2:151). This verse highlights the multifaceted role of prophets in education, purification, and spiritual enlightenment.

The theological foundation of prophethood rests on the belief that Allah, in His mercy and wisdom, provides guidance to ensure that humanity can navigate the complexities of life and fulfil their purpose. Prophethood bridges the gap between the divine and the human, making the principles of ultimate reality accessible and comprehensible to all.

The Characteristics and Functions of Prophets

Prophets possess unique characteristics that distinguish them as trustworthy and capable messengers of Allah. Some of the key attributes include:

1. Truthfulness (Sidq): Prophets are inherently truthful and honest, ensuring that their messages are free from falsehood and deceit.
2. Integrity (Amanah): They are entrusted with divine revelation and carry out their duties with utmost integrity and responsibility.
3. Intellect (Aql): Prophets possess keen intellect and wisdom, enabling them to understand and convey complex theological and moral principles.
4. Patience (Sabr): They exhibit patience and perseverance in the face of adversity and opposition, steadfastly delivering their messages despite challenges.
5. Compassion (Rahmah): Prophets demonstrate profound compassion and concern for their communities, striving to guide them towards righteousness and salvation.

The functions of prophets encompass several key roles, including:

1. Revelation: Prophets receive and convey divine revelation, making known the will of Allah and providing guidance on matters of faith, law, and ethics.
2. Moral Exemplars: They serve as role models, embodying the principles of Tawhid and demonstrating how to live a life aligned with divine will.
3. Social Reformers: Prophets address social injustices and inequalities, advocating for the rights of the oppressed and promoting justice, equity, and compassion.
4. Spiritual Guides: They provide spiritual guidance, helping individuals cultivate a deeper connection with Allah and achieve spiritual growth and purification.
5. Warner and Bearer of Glad Tidings: Prophets warn of the consequences of disobedience and disbelief while offering hope and encouragement to those who follow divine guidance.

The Universality of Prophethood

The Quran asserts the universality of prophethood, stating that Allah has sent messengers to every nation throughout history. Verses such as, "And We certainly sent into every nation a messenger, [saying], 'Worship Allah and avoid Taghut'" (Quran 16:36), highlight that divine guidance is accessible to all humanity, regardless of time or place. This universality reflects Allah's justice and mercy, ensuring that every community receives the opportunity to understand and follow His guidance.

The Quran mentions several prophets by name, including Adam, Noah, Abraham, Moses, Jesus, and Muhammad (peace be upon them all), each of whom played a pivotal role in conveying Allah's message and guiding their respective communities. The diversity of prophets and their missions underscores the adaptability and relevance of divine guidance across different cultures and historical contexts.

The Seal of Prophethood: Muhammad (PBUH)

The Quran identifies Muhammad (PBUH) as the final prophet, referred to as the "Seal of the Prophets" (Khatam an-Nabiyyin). His prophethood marks the culmination of the prophetic tradition, and his message is considered universal and final. The Quran states, "Muhammad is not the father of [any] one of your men, but [he is] the Messenger of Allah and Seal of the Prophets. And ever is Allah, of all things, Knowing" (Quran 33:40).

Muhammad's prophethood is characterized by the comprehensive and timeless nature of his message, which addresses all aspects of human life, including theology, law, ethics, and spirituality. The Quran, as the final revelation, serves as a complete and enduring guide for humanity, offering solutions to contemporary challenges and providing a framework for spiritual and moral development.

The Quran as a Guide

The Quran, revealed to Muhammad (PBUH), serves as the ultimate guide for humanity, offering insights into the nature of ultimate reality and the principles that govern existence. It provides detailed instructions on worship, ethical conduct, social justice, and spiritual growth, making it a comprehensive source of divine guidance. The Quran states, "This is the Book about which there is no doubt, a guidance for those conscious of Allah" (Quran 2:2).

The Quran's guidance is not limited to religious rituals but extends to all areas of life, encouraging believers to reflect on its teachings and apply them in their daily lives. Verses such as, "And We have certainly made the Quran easy for remembrance, so is there any who will remember?" (Quran 54:17), emphasize the accessibility and relevance of the Quran's message.

The Role of Sunnah

In addition to the Quran, the Sunnah (the practices and teachings of Muhammad (PBUH)) provides essential guidance for understanding and implementing Islamic principles. The Sunnah complements the Quran, offering practical examples of how to live according to divine guidance. The Quran instructs believers to follow the Prophet's example: "There has certainly been for you in the Messenger of Allah an excellent pattern for anyone whose hope is in Allah and the Last Day and [who] remembers Allah often" (Quran 33:21).

The Sunnah encompasses various aspects of the Prophet's life, including his words (Hadith), actions, and approvals. It serves as a vital source of knowledge for interpreting the Quran and applying its teachings in diverse contexts. The Hadith literature, meticulously preserved and authenticated, provides valuable insights into the Prophet's character, wisdom, and leadership, making it an indispensable part of Islamic tradition.

The Impact of Prophethood on Human Life and Society

The institution of prophethood has a profound impact on human life and society, shaping moral values, social norms, and cultural practices. Prophets serve as catalysts for positive change, addressing moral corruption, social injustice, and spiritual ignorance. Their messages inspire individuals and communities to strive for higher ideals, fostering a sense of purpose, accountability, and devotion to Allah.

The ethical teachings of prophets promote values such as honesty, integrity, compassion, and justice, which are essential for building harmonious and just societies. By advocating for the rights of the marginalized and oppressed, prophets challenge entrenched systems of injustice and inequality, paving the way for social reform and transformation.

The spiritual guidance provided by prophets helps individuals cultivate a deeper connection with Allah, achieve personal growth, and attain inner peace. Through their teachings and examples, prophets illuminate the path to spiritual enlightenment, encouraging believers to seek divine closeness and ultimate salvation.

The Eschatological Role of Prophethood

The Quran emphasizes the eschatological significance of prophethood, highlighting the role of prophets in preparing humanity for the Day of Judgment (Yawm al-Qiyamah). Prophets warn of the consequences of disbelief and disobedience, urging people to repent and follow divine guidance to attain salvation. Verses such as, "Indeed, We have sent to you a Messenger as a witness upon you just as We sent to Pharaoh a messenger. But Pharaoh disobeyed the messenger, so We seized him with a ruinous seizure" (Quran 73:15-16), underscore the importance of heeding prophetic warnings.

The eschatological dimension of prophethood reinforces the belief in divine justice and accountability, encouraging individuals to live righteously and prepare for the hereafter. Prophets provide assurance of Allah's mercy and forgiveness for those who repent and follow His guidance, offering hope and encouragement in the face of life's challenges.

The Spiritual Benefits of Following Prophetic Guidance

Following prophetic guidance offers numerous spiritual benefits, enhancing one's faith, character, and sense of purpose. By emulating the prophets, believers can cultivate virtues such as patience, humility, and sincerity, which are essential for spiritual growth and closeness to Allah. The Quran states, "And whoever obeys Allah and His Messenger has certainly attained a great attainment" (Quran 33:71).

The teachings of prophets provide a framework for navigating the complexities of life, offering practical solutions to moral dilemmas and ethical challenges. By adhering to prophetic guidance, individuals can lead balanced and fulfilling lives, characterized by devotion to Allah, compassionate interactions, and social responsibility.

The spiritual benefits of following prophetic guidance extend to the afterlife, where adherence to divine principles is rewarded with eternal bliss in Paradise (Jannah). The Quran describes the ultimate reward for the righteous: "But those who believed and did righteous deeds will have gardens beneath which rivers flow. That is the great attainment" (Quran 85:11).

Conclusion: Embracing the Role of Prophethood

The concept of prophethood, as presented in the Quran, offers a comprehensive and profound understanding of divine guidance and its significance for human life and spirituality.

CHAPTER 14

The Quran as a Metaphysical Guide

Introduction to the Quran as a Metaphysical Guide

The Quran, as the final revelation of Allah SWT, serves not only as a spiritual and moral guide but also as a profound metaphysical guide. It provides insights into the nature of reality, the principles governing the universe, and the purpose of human existence. This chapter delves into the Quranic perspective on metaphysics, exploring how the Quran guides believers in understanding the unseen dimensions of reality, the nature of existence, and the relationship between the Creator and creation. By examining the metaphysical teachings of the Quran, we aim to uncover the deeper layers of meaning and wisdom that underpin its guidance.

The Nature of Existence and Reality

The Quran presents a comprehensive view of existence and reality, emphasizing the interconnectedness and purposefulness of creation. It asserts that all that exists is a manifestation of Allah's will and power. Verses such as, "Allah is the Creator of all things, and He is, over all things, Disposer of affairs" (Quran 39:62), highlight the divine origin and sustenance of the universe.

The Quranic concept of reality encompasses both the seen (al-shahada) and the unseen (al-ghayb) realms. The seen realm includes the physical world, which is accessible to human perception and scientific inquiry. The unseen realm, however, encompasses metaphysical dimensions that lie beyond sensory perception, including the existence of angels, jinn, the soul, and the hereafter. Belief in the unseen is a fundamental aspect of faith, as emphasized in the verse, "This is the Book about which there is no doubt, a guidance for those conscious of Allah – who believe in the unseen, establish prayer, and spend out of what We have provided for them" (Quran 2:2-3).

The Relationship Between Creator and Creation

The Quran provides a detailed account of the relationship between the Creator and creation, emphasizing Allah's sovereignty, wisdom, and mercy. Allah is depicted as the ultimate source of all existence, whose will and knowledge encompass everything. The Quran states, "To Allah belongs whatever is in the heavens and whatever is in the earth. Whether you show what is within yourselves or conceal it, Allah will bring you to account for it" (Quran 2:284).

This relationship is characterized by a dynamic interplay between divine decree (qadar) and human free will (ikhtiyar). While Allah's will governs the overall order of the universe, humans are endowed with the capacity to make choices and are held accountable for their actions. The Quranic perspective emphasizes that human actions are meaningful and consequential, yet they unfold within the framework of divine wisdom and justice. Verses such as, "And say, 'The truth is from your Lord, so whoever wills – let him believe; and whoever wills – let him disbelieve'" (Quran 18:29), underscore the principle of free will while affirming divine sovereignty.

The Purpose and Order of Creation

The Quran asserts that creation is purposeful and orderly, reflecting Allah's wisdom and benevolence. The natural world, with its intricate balance and harmony, serves as a testament to the divine order. The Quran invites believers to reflect on the signs of Allah in creation, stating, "Indeed, in the creation of the heavens and the earth and the alternation of the night and the day are signs for those of understanding" (Quran 3:190).

The purpose of creation, according to the Quran, is to worship and serve Allah. This purpose is articulated in the verse, "And I did not create the jinn and mankind except to worship Me" (Quran 51:56). Worship in this context encompasses not only ritual acts but also living in accordance with divine guidance, striving for moral and spiritual excellence, and contributing to the well-being of others.

The Quranic concept of order extends to the moral and ethical dimensions of human life. It provides a comprehensive framework for ethical conduct, emphasizing principles such as justice, compassion, truthfulness, and responsibility. By adhering to these principles, believers align themselves with the divine order and fulfil their purpose in creation.

The Metaphysical Dimensions of Time and Space

The Quran offers profound insights into the metaphysical dimensions of time and space, challenging conventional understandings and inviting believers to contemplate their deeper meanings. Time, in the Quranic perspective, is both linear and cyclical, encompassing the temporal sequence of events as well as the recurring patterns in nature. The Quran states, "He created the heavens and earth in truth. He wraps the night over the day and wraps the day over the night and has subjected the sun and the moon, each running [its course] for a specified term" (Quran 39:5).

This verse highlights the regularity and precision of celestial movements, reflecting the disciplined nature of divine creation. The Quran also alludes to the relativity of time, suggesting that divine time operates on a different scale than human time. Verses such as, "A day with your Lord is like a thousand years of what you count" (Quran 22:47), invite believers to expand their understanding of time and recognize the limitations of human perception.

Space, in the Quranic view, is not merely a physical expanse but a dynamic and purposeful creation. The Quran describes the heavens and the earth as signs of Allah's power and wisdom, inviting contemplation and reflection. Verses such as, "Do you not see that Allah has created the heavens and the earth in truth? If He wills, He can do away with you and produce a new creation" (Quran 14:19), emphasize the vastness and grandeur of the cosmos, underscoring the transient nature of physical existence and the enduring reality of the divine.

The Journey of the Soul

The Quran provides a detailed account of the soul's journey, encompassing its origin, life experiences, and ultimate destiny. The soul (ruh) is described as a divine creation, breathed into the human body by Allah. This divine origin is emphasized in the verse, "And when I have proportioned him and breathed into him of My [created] soul, then fall down to him in prostration" (Quran 15:29). The soul's journey begins with its creation and entry into the physical body, followed by a series of stages that include life, death, the intermediate realm (Barzakh), and the hereafter (Akhirah).

The Quran teaches that the soul's ultimate purpose is to worship and serve Allah, striving for spiritual growth and purification. This journey involves continuous striving and self-improvement, as emphasized in the verse, "And that there is not for man except that [good] for which he strives and that his effort is going to be seen" (Quran 53:39-40). The soul's journey is marked by trials and challenges, which serve as tests of faith and opportunities for spiritual development.

The Quran also describes the ultimate destiny of the soul, emphasizing the eternal nature of the hereafter. The Day of Judgment (Yawm al-Qiyamah) is depicted as a time when all souls will be resurrected and held accountable for their actions. Verses such as, "The Day when mankind will stand before the Lord of the worlds?" (Quran 83:6), highlight the significance of this event and the realization of divine justice. The ultimate reward for the righteous is eternal bliss in Paradise (Jannah), while the wicked face punishment in Hell (Jahannam). The Quran provides vivid descriptions of these abodes, emphasizing the consequences of one's actions and the fulfilment of divine promise.

The Interplay Between Knowledge and Faith

The Quran emphasizes the interplay between knowledge ('ilm) and faith (iman), highlighting their complementary roles in understanding ultimate reality. Knowledge, in the Quranic perspective, is not limited to empirical observation but encompasses a deeper awareness of the metaphysical dimensions of existence. The pursuit of knowledge is seen as a means of gaining insights into the divine order and strengthening one's faith. Verses such as, "Say, 'Are those who know equal to those who do not know?' Only they will remember [who are] people of understanding" (Quran 39:9), underscore the value of knowledge and its role in spiritual growth.

Faith, on the other hand, involves accepting the realities of the unseen and trusting in Allah's wisdom and guidance. The Quran teaches that true faith encompasses both belief in the unseen and adherence to divine commands. Verses such as, "O you who have believed, believe in Allah and His Messenger and the Book that He sent down upon His Messenger and the Scripture which He sent down before. And whoever disbelieves in Allah, His angels, His books, His messengers, and the Last Day has certainly gone far astray" (Quran 4:136), highlight the integral connection between knowledge and faith.

The Quran encourages believers to seek knowledge, reflect on its teachings, and apply them in their daily lives. This process of integrating knowledge and faith leads to a deeper understanding of ultimate reality and a more profound connection with Allah. By harmonizing knowledge and faith, believers can navigate the complexities of life with confidence and resilience, guided by the principles of divine wisdom and justice.

The Ethical and Moral Dimensions of the Quran

The Quran provides a comprehensive framework for ethical and moral conduct, emphasizing principles such as justice, compassion, truthfulness, and responsibility. These principles are not merely abstract ideals but are deeply rooted in the metaphysical understanding of ultimate reality. By adhering to these ethical guidelines, believers align themselves with the divine order and fulfil their purpose in creation.

Justice (adl) is a central principle of Quranic ethics, reflecting Allah's attribute of being the Just (Al-Adl). The Quran states, "O you who have believed, be persistently standing firm in justice, witnesses for Allah, even if it be against yourselves or parents and relatives" (Quran 4:135).

CHAPTER 15

The Interconnectedness of All Creation

Introduction to the Interconnectedness of Creation

The concept of interconnectedness is fundamental to understanding the Quranic perspective on creation. The Quran presents the universe as a meticulously ordered and interdependent system, reflecting the unity and harmony of Allah's design. This chapter delves into the Quranic teachings on the interconnectedness of all creation, exploring its theological, ecological, and ethical dimensions. By examining the intricate relationships between different elements of creation, we aim to uncover the profound wisdom and balance that characterize the divine order.

The Unity of Allah and the Unity of Creation

The Quran emphasizes the unity of Allah (Tawhid) as the foundational principle of existence. This unity is mirrored in the interconnectedness of creation, where every element is part of a larger, harmonious whole. The Quran states, "To Allah belongs whatever is in the heavens and whatever is in the earth. And He is the Most High, the Most Great" (Quran 42:4). This verse underscores that all creation belongs to Allah and operates under His sovereign command.

The concept of Tawhid extends beyond theological assertions to encompass a holistic understanding of reality. The unity of Allah implies that the universe is not a collection of random or isolated entities but a coherent and purposeful system. This interconnectedness reflects the divine wisdom and meticulous planning that underlie every aspect of creation.

The Signs of Interconnectedness in Nature

The natural world provides abundant signs (ayat) of the interconnectedness of creation. The Quran frequently invites believers to observe and reflect upon these signs, recognizing them as manifestations of Allah's power and wisdom. Verses such as, "And it is He who created the night and the day and the sun and the moon; all [heavenly bodies] swim along, each in its rounded course" (Quran 21:33), highlight the precise and interdependent movements of celestial bodies.

The Quran also describes the interdependence of living organisms and their environments. The water cycle, for instance, is presented as a sign of divine provision and interconnectedness: "And We sent down rain from the sky and made grow thereby gardens and grain from the harvest" (Quran 50:9). This verse illustrates how water, a fundamental resource, sustains plant life, which in turn supports animal and human life.

The interconnectedness of ecosystems is further emphasized in the Quran's depiction of the balance (mizan) that Allah has established in creation. Verses such as, "And the heaven

He raised and imposed the balance. That you not transgress within the balance. And establish weight in justice and do not make deficient the balance" (Quran 55:7-9), underscore the importance of maintaining harmony and balance in the natural world. This balance is not merely ecological but also moral and ethical, reflecting the comprehensive nature of divine order.

The Human Role in the Web of Life

The Quran assigns humans a unique role within the interconnected web of life, emphasizing their responsibility as stewards (khalifah) of the earth. This stewardship entails recognizing and respecting the interconnectedness of all creation, acting with justice and compassion towards other beings. The Quran states, "It is He who has made you successors upon the earth and has raised some of you above others in degrees [of rank] that He may try you through what He has given you" (Quran 6:165). This verse highlights the moral and ethical dimensions of human stewardship.

Human actions have significant impacts on the natural world, and the Quran warns against corruption and exploitation that disrupt the balance of creation. Verses such as, "Corruption has appeared throughout the land and sea by [reason of] what the hands of people have earned so He may let them taste part of [the consequence of] what they have done that perhaps they will return [to righteousness]" (Quran 30:41), serve as reminders of the consequences of human misconduct.

The Quran encourages sustainable practices and ethical treatment of the environment, promoting a sense of reverence and gratitude towards Allah's creation. By fulfilling their role as stewards, humans can contribute to the preservation and enhancement of the natural world, aligning their actions with the principles of divine wisdom and justice.

The Ethical Implications of Interconnectedness

The interconnectedness of creation has profound ethical implications, shaping how individuals interact with each other and with the environment. The Quranic teachings on justice (adl), compassion (rahmah), and responsibility (amanah) are rooted in the recognition of this interconnectedness. By adhering to these ethical principles, believers can foster harmonious relationships and contribute to the well-being of all creation.

Justice, as a core ethical principle, requires acknowledging and respecting the rights and needs of others. The Quran emphasizes the importance of justice in all interactions, stating, "O you who have believed, be persistently standing firm in justice, witnesses for Allah, even if it be against yourselves or parents and relatives" (Quran 4:135). This verse underscores the universality and impartiality of justice, which must be upheld to maintain harmony and balance.

Compassion is another key ethical principle that reflects the interconnectedness of creation. The Quran encourages believers to show kindness and care towards others, particularly the vulnerable and disadvantaged. Verses such as, "And lower to them the wing of humility out of mercy and say, 'My Lord, have mercy upon them as they brought me up [when I was] small'" (Quran 17:24), highlight the importance of compassion in familial and social relationships.

Responsibility, as an ethical principle, entails recognizing one's role and duties within the interconnected web of life. The Quran teaches that humans are entrusted with the care of the earth and its inhabitants, and they will be held accountable for their actions. Verses such as, "Indeed, We offered the Trust to the heavens and the earth and the mountains, and they declined to bear it and feared it; but man [undertook to] bear it. Indeed, he was unjust and ignorant" (Quran 33:72), highlight the gravity of this responsibility and the need for conscientious stewardship.

The Spiritual Dimensions of Interconnectedness

The recognition of interconnectedness also has profound spiritual dimensions, fostering a deeper sense of unity, humility, and gratitude. The Quran teaches that all creation is engaged in the worship and glorification of Allah, reflecting a universal sense of purpose and devotion. Verses such as, "The seven heavens and the earth and whatever is in them exalt Him. And there is not a thing except that it exalts [Allah] by His praise, but you do not understand their [way of] exalting. Indeed, He is ever Forbearing and Forgiving" (Quran 17:44), emphasize the universal nature of worship and the interconnectedness of all beings in their relationship with the Creator.

This spiritual interconnectedness invites believers to see themselves as part of a larger, divine tapestry, where every element has a role and purpose. It fosters a sense of humility, as individuals recognize their dependence on Allah and the interconnected web of life. It also encourages gratitude, as believers appreciate the blessings and provisions that Allah has bestowed upon all creation.

By embracing the spiritual dimensions of interconnectedness, believers can cultivate a deeper sense of reverence and devotion, aligning their actions with the principles of divine wisdom and justice. This spiritual awareness enhances one's connection with Allah and contributes to personal and communal well-being.

The Eschatological Vision of Interconnectedness

The Quran presents an eschatological vision that underscores the interconnectedness of all creation and the realization of divine justice. The Day of Judgment (Yawm al-Qiyamah) is depicted as a time when the true nature of existence is fully revealed, and the interconnectedness of actions and their consequences is made manifest. Verses such as, "So whoever does an atom's weight of good will see it, and whoever does an atom's weight of evil will see it" (Quran 99:7-8), highlight the meticulous nature of divine justice and the interconnectedness of deeds and their outcomes.

This eschatological perspective reinforces the importance of living a righteous life, guided by the principles of Tawhid and divine guidance. It emphasizes that every action, no matter how small, has significance and contributes to the overall balance and harmony of creation. The ultimate reward for the righteous is eternal bliss in Paradise (Jannah), where the interconnectedness of all creation is experienced in its most perfect and harmonious form.

The Quran provides vivid descriptions of Paradise, emphasizing the interconnectedness of its inhabitants and the harmony that characterizes this eternal abode. Verses such as, "Gardens of perpetual residence, which they will enter, beneath which rivers flow. They will have therein whatever they wish. Thus does Allah reward the righteous" (Quran 16:31), depict a vision of interconnected bliss, where all beings coexist in peace and fulfilment.

Conclusion: Embracing the Interconnectedness of Creation

The Quranic teachings on the interconnectedness of creation offer a profound and holistic understanding of reality. By recognizing the unity and harmony that characterize the divine order, believers are invited to see themselves as part of a larger, purposeful system. This recognition fosters a sense of responsibility, compassion, and reverence, guiding individuals to live in accordance with the principles of divine wisdom and justice.

As we conclude our metaphysical odyssey, we are called to reflect on the interconnectedness of all creation and embrace the ethical and spiritual dimensions of this understanding. By aligning our actions with the principles of Tawhid, justice, and compassion, we can contribute to the well-being of all creation and fulfil our role as stewards of the earth. This journey towards understanding and embodying the interconnectedness of creation leads to intellectual enlightenment, spiritual fulfilment, and a profound connection with the Creator.

OVERALL CONCLUSION

The Metaphysical Odyssey

The Journey Through the Veil

"Beyond the Veil: A Metaphysical Odyssey" has guided us through an intricate exploration of reality, as understood through the lens of the Quran. Our journey has delved into the profound depths of metaphysical concepts, bridging the seen and unseen, the material and the spiritual. We have traversed through the essence of divine justice, discipline, the nature of time and space, the soul's journey, and the ultimate reality of Allah's oneness. Along this odyssey, the Quran has served as our compass, revealing the layers of existence and offering a holistic framework for understanding the universe and our place within it.

The Unity of Existence

A central theme that has emerged from our exploration is the unity and interconnectedness of all existence. The concept of Tawhid, the oneness of Allah, permeates every aspect of creation, emphasizing that all things are interconnected and part of a greater, harmonious whole. This unity is reflected in the natural order, the balance of ecosystems, and the intricate relationships between living beings. The recognition of this interconnectedness invites us to see beyond the surface of material reality and appreciate the deeper, underlying principles that govern the cosmos.

The Role of Divine Guidance

The Quran, as the final revelation, provides a comprehensive guide to navigating the complexities of life and understanding the metaphysical dimensions of existence. It offers detailed teachings on worship, ethics, social justice, and spiritual growth, illuminating the path to divine closeness and ultimate fulfilment. The prophetic tradition, embodied by Muhammad (PBUH), serves as a practical model for living in accordance with divine guidance, demonstrating how to integrate knowledge, faith, and ethical conduct in everyday life.

The Balance Between Free Will and Divine Will

Our exploration has highlighted the dynamic interplay between free will and divine will. While Allah's sovereignty encompasses all things, humans are endowed with the capacity to make choices and are held accountable for their actions. This balance ensures that human life is meaningful and that our actions have real consequences, both in this world and the hereafter. The Quran teaches that by aligning our free will with divine guidance, we can achieve a state of harmony with the divine order and fulfil our purpose as Allah's servants.

The Importance of Ethical and Moral Conduct

The Quranic teachings on justice, compassion, and responsibility underscore the importance of ethical and moral conduct in achieving a balanced and harmonious existence. By adhering to these principles, we contribute to the well-being of society and the preservation of the natural world. The Quran calls us to act with integrity, fairness, and kindness, recognizing the rights and dignity of all beings. This ethical framework is not only a guide for individual conduct but also a foundation for building just and compassionate communities.

The Spiritual Dimensions of Existence

Our journey has revealed the profound spiritual dimensions of existence, emphasizing the significance of inner growth and spiritual awareness. The Quran teaches that true fulfilment and peace come from a deep connection with Allah and a sincere commitment to worship and ethical conduct. Spiritual practices such as prayer, fasting, and remembrance cultivate mindfulness, humility, and devotion, fostering a sense of divine presence in our lives.

The recognition of the soul's journey and the eschatological realities of the hereafter further deepen our understanding of existence. The Quranic vision of the afterlife underscores the eternal consequences of our actions and the ultimate realization of divine justice. This eschatological perspective encourages us to live with a sense of purpose and accountability, striving for righteousness and seeking Allah's mercy.

The Intellectual and Spiritual Synthesis

"Beyond the Veil" has aimed to synthesize intellectual inquiry and spiritual reflection, demonstrating that the pursuit of knowledge and the cultivation of faith are complementary endeavours. The Quran encourages the use of intellect to reflect on divine signs and seek understanding, while also emphasizing the importance of faith in accepting the unseen realities. This synthesis fosters a holistic approach to life, where rational thought and spiritual insight coexist and reinforce each other.

The Call to Action

As we conclude our metaphysical odyssey, we are called to embody the principles and insights gained from our exploration. The Quran invites us to live with a sense of purpose, guided by the knowledge of ultimate reality and the awareness of our interconnectedness with all creation. By striving for justice, compassion, and spiritual growth, we can contribute to the flourishing of humanity and the preservation of the natural world.

This journey is not merely an intellectual exercise but a transformative process that shapes our character, actions, and relationships. It calls us to integrate the wisdom of the Quran into our daily lives, fostering a deeper connection with Allah and a more profound appreciation of the divine order.

A Journey Without End

The quest for understanding ultimate reality is an ongoing journey, one that continues beyond the pages of this book. The

Quran offers an inexhaustible source of wisdom and guidance, inviting us to delve deeper into its teachings and reflect on its meanings. Each reflection and act of worship brings us closer to the divine, unveiling new layers of insight and understanding.

In this continuous journey, we are reminded of the words of the Quran: "And those who strive for Us – We will surely guide them to Our ways. And indeed, Allah is with the doers of good" (Quran 29:69). This verse encapsulates the essence of our odyssey, emphasizing that sincere effort and commitment to righteousness are met with divine guidance and support.

As we move forward, may we carry with us the insights and lessons from our exploration, allowing them to illuminate our path and deepen our connection with the Creator. May this journey lead to intellectual enlightenment, spiritual fulfilment, and a more profound understanding of the ultimate reality that binds us all.

Embracing the Ultimate Reality

In embracing the ultimate reality as revealed in the Quran, we recognize the infinite compassion, wisdom, and justice of Allah SWT. We acknowledge our place within the divine order, our responsibilities as stewards of the earth, and our potential for spiritual growth and transformation. This recognition inspires a life of purpose, devotion, and ethical conduct, aligned with the principles of Tawhid.

"Beyond the Veil: A Metaphysical Odyssey" is an invitation to continue this journey of discovery, reflection, and action. It is a call to transcend the limitations of material existence and embrace the profound truths that lie beyond the veil. May this odyssey inspire us to seek knowledge, cultivate faith, and strive for righteousness, ultimately leading us to the realization of our true purpose and the fulfilment of our highest potential as servants of Allah.

CURRICULUM VITAE

PROFESSOR DR. KAMIL IDRIS

Former Director General (elected by the Coordination Committee and the General Assembly)

World Intellectual Property Organization
(WIPO), United Nations Specialised Agency

**Former Secretary-General
(elected by the Council)**

International Union for the Protection of New Varieties of Plants
(UPOV)

Former Member (elected by the United Nations General Assembly)

United Nations International Law
Commission (ILC)

Former Ambassador

Former President

World Arbitration and Mediation Court (WAMC)

Member

Permanent Court of Arbitration (PCA),The Hague

President

The International Court of Arbitration and Mediation (ICAM)

Chairman

Board of Trustees of the Union of the Afro-Asian Universities

Academic Distinctions

LLB (Law), University of Khartoum (Honors)

Bachelor of Arts, Philosophical Studies, University of Cairo (Honors)

Diploma, Public Administration (Management Department), Institute of Public Administration, Khartoum

Master in International Affairs (MAIA), University of Ohio, USA (First Class Average)

Doctorate (PhD) in International Law, Graduate Institute of International Studies, University of Geneva (Distinction)

Doctorate Thesis: "Case study on the Treaty Establishing a Preferential Trade Area for Eastern and Southern African States"

Academic Interests

Certificates
International Economics, Graduate Institute of International Studies (Geneva)

International History and Political Science, Graduate Institute of International Studies (Geneva)

International Law of Development, Graduate Institute of International Studies (Geneva)

The Law of International Waterways, Graduate Institute of International Studies (Geneva)

International Law of Financing and Banking Systems, Graduate Institute of International Studies (Geneva)

Languages
Arabic, English, French, Spanish (good knowledge)

Teaching
Lecturer in Philosophy and Jurisprudence,

University of Cairo (1976-1977)

Lecturer in Jurisprudence, Ohio University, USA (1978)

External Examiner in International Law, Faculty of Law, University of Khartoum (1984)

Lecturer in Intellectual Property Law, Faculty of Law, University of Khartoum (1986)

Lecturer in several international, regional and national seminars, workshops and symposia

Member, International Association for the Advancement of Teaching and Research in Intellectual Property Law (ATRIP)

Decorations
Awarded the Scholars and Researchers State Gold Medal, presented by the President of the Republic of the Sudan (1983)

Awarded the Scholars and Researchers Gold Medal, presented by the President of the Academy of Scientific Research and Technology of Egypt (1985)

Awarded the decoration of the Commandeur de l'Ordre national du Lion, Senegal (1998)

Awarded the Medal of the Bolshoi Theatre, presented by the Director of the Bolshoi Theatre, Russian Federation (1999)

Awarded the Honorary Medal, presented by the Rector of the Moscow State Institute of International Relations, Russian Federation (1999)

Awarded the Honorary Medal of The Gulf Cooperation Council (GCC), Saudi Arabia (1999)

Awarded the Golden Plaque of the Town of Banská Bystrica, presented by the Mayor of Banská Bystrica, Slovakia (1999)

Awarded the Golden Medal of Matej Bel University, presented by the Dean of the University, Banská Bystrica, Slovakia (1999)

Awarded the Silver Jubilee Medal of the Eurasian Patent Organization (EAPO), presented by Mr. Viktor Blinnikov, President of the Eurasian Patent Office, Russian Federation (2000)

Award of Distinguished Merit, presented by the Egyptian Supreme Council for Science and Technology, Egypt (2000)

Awarded a Plaque from the Syrian Inventors' Association, Syrian Arab Republic (2000)

Awarded the Grand Cross of the Infante D. Enrique, Portugal (2001)

Awarded a Medal from the People's Assembly of Egypt, Egypt (2001)

Awarded a Medal from the Constitutional Court of Romania, Romania (2001)

Awarded a Medal from the Parliament of Romania, Romania (2001)

Awarded the Golden Medal Dolores del Río al Mérito internacional en favor de los derechos de los artistas intérpretes from the National Association of Interpreters (ANDI), Mexico (2001)

Awarded the Golden Medal from The State Agency on Industrial Property Protection, Republic of Moldova (2001)

Awarded the decoration of the Commandeur de l'Ordre du Mérite national, Côte d'Ivoire (2002)

Awarded the Maria Sklodowska-Curie Medal from the Association of Polish Inventors and Rationalizers, Poland (2002)

Awarded the decoration of The Order of the Two Niles, First Class, from the President of the Republic of Sudan, Sudan (2002)

Kamil Idris Library, University of Juba, Sudan (2002)

Kamil Idris Conference Hall, Intellectual Property Court, The Judiciary, Sudan (2002)

Awarded the Dank Medal (medal of glory), from the President of the Kyrgyz Republic, Kyrgyzstan (2003)

Award from the University of National and World Economy, Bulgaria (2003)

"Venice Award for Intellectual Property", presented by the Mayor of Venice (2004)

Awarded the Medal of Oman, presented by His Royal Highness Fahid Bin Mahmud Al-Said, Deputy Prime Minister of the Council of Ministers, Oman (2004)

Awarded the decoration of the Aztec Eagle, presented by Ambassador Luis Alfonso de Alba (Permanent Representative of Mexico to International Organizations in Geneva) on behalf of Presidente of Mexico Vicente Fox, (2005)

Kamil Idris Building, Regional Training Center, African Regional Intellectual Property Organization (ARIPO), Harare, Zimbabwe (2006)

Awarded a Medal commemorating the 60 years of the United Nations, Bulgaria (2006)

Awarded a Medal commemorating the 60 years of the Independence of Jordan, Jordan (2006)

Award of Distinguished Leadership presented by the International Publishers'Association (IPA) and the Arab Publishers Association, Egypt (2007)

Awarded a Medal on the occasion of the Fujairah International Monodrama Festival, Fujairah,United Arab Emirates (2007)

Awarded a Medal on the occasion of the Intellectual Property Day presented by The Regional Institute for Intellectual Property of the Faculty of Law, University of Helwan, Egypt (2008)

Awarded The Distinguished Medal of Cultural Innovation, Sudan (2008)

Awarded The Family Club Decoration, Sudan (2008)

Awarded The World Intellectual Property Organization (WIPO) Medal, Geneva, Switzerland (2008)

Awarded The International Union Of The Protection Of New Varieties Of Plants (UPOV)

Medal, Geneva, Switzerland (2008)

Awarded The Distinguished Medal Of The Sudanese Centre Of Intellectual Property, Khartoum, Sudan (2009)

Awarded The Medal Of Kenana sugar Company, Khartoum, Sudan (2009)

Awarded The Decoration Of Loyalty And Gratitude Of Omdurman National Broadcasting Station, Sudan (2010)

Awarded The decoration (WISHAH) of the Syrian revolution (2013)

Awarded The decoration (WISHAH) of Rashid Diab cultural center, Khartoum, Sudan (2013)

Awarded The Medal of Distinction by the International Association of Muslim

Lawyers (2014)

Honorary Degrees

1999 Honorary Professor of Law, Peking University, China

1999 Doctor Honoris Causa, The Doctor's Council of the State University of Moldova, Republic of Moldova

1999 Doctor Honoris Causa, Franklin Pierce Law Center (Concord, New Hampshire), United States of America

1999 Doctor Honoris Causa, Fudan University (Shanghai), China

2000 Doctor Honoris Causa, University of National and World Economy (Sofia), Bulgaria

2001 Doctor Honoris Causa, University of Bucharest, Romania

2001 Doctor Honoris Causa, Hannam University (Daejeon), Republic of Korea

2001 Doctor Honoris Causa, Mongolian University of Science and Technology (Ulaanbaatar), Mongolia

2001 Doctor Honoris Causa, Matej Bel University (Banská Bystrica), Slovakia

2002 Doctor Honoris Causa, National Technical University of Ukraine "Kyiv Polytechnic Institute" (Kyiv), Ukraine

2003 Doctor Honoris Causa, Al Eman Al Mahdi University (White Nile State), Sudan

2005 Degree of Doctor of Letters (Honoris Causa), Indira Gandhi National Open University (IGNOU), India

2005 Doctor Honoris Causa, Latvian Academy of Sciences, Latvia

2006 Doctor Honoris Causa, University of Azerbaijan, Azerbaijan

2007 Doctor Honoris Causa, University of Al-Gezira, Sudan

2007 Doctor of International Law and Honorary Professor, Belarussian State University, Belarus

2007 Doctor Honoris Causa, University of Khartoum, Sudan

2007 Doctor Honoris Causa, Ss. Cyril and Methodius University (Skopje), The Former Yugoslav Republic of Macedonia

2008 Doctor Honoris Causa, Kyrgyz State University of Construction, Transport and Architecture (Bishkek), Kyrgystan

2008 Certificate of Appreciation, Ahlia University, Khartoum, Sudan

2020 Honorary Professor, Durham University (United Kingdom)

Experience

Professional
Part-time Journalist, El-Ayam and El-Sahafa (Sudanese) newspapers (1971-1979)

Lecturer, University of Cairo (1976)

Assistant Director, Arab Department, Ministry of Foreign Affairs, Khartoum (1977)

Assistant Director, Research Department, Ministry of Foreign Affairs, Khartoum (January-June 1978)

Deputy Director, Legal Department, Ministry of Foreign Affairs, Khartoum (July-December 1978)

Member of Sudan Permanent Mission to the United Nations Office, Geneva (1979-1982)

Vice-Consul of Sudan in Switzerland (1979-1982)

Legal Adviser of Sudan Permanent Mission to the United Nations Office, Geneva (1979-1982)

Senior Program Officer, Development Cooperation and External Relations Bureau for Africa, World Intellectual Property Organization (WIPO), (1982-1985)

Director, Development Cooperation and External Relations Bureau for Arab and Central and Eastern European Countries, WIPO (1985-1994)

Ambassador, Ministry of Foreign Affairs, Sudan (current status at national level)

Deputy Director General, WIPO (1994-1997)

Director General, WIPO, since 1997

Secretary-General, International Union for the Protection of Plant Varieties (UPOV), since 1997

Special

External Assessor for the title of Professor, College of Islamic Studies (CIS), Sheikh Hamad University, Doha, Qatar 2024

Member of The Academic Council, University of Khartoum (Sudan, April 2007)

Member, Board of Trustees, Nile Valley University (Egypt, June 2000)

Member, United Nations International Law Commission (ILC) (2000-2001)

Member, Advisory Council on Intellectual Property (ACIP), Franklin Pierce Law Center (Concord, New Hampshire, 1999)

Member, United Nations International Law Commission (ILC) (1992-1996)

Vice-Chairman of the International Law Commission (ILC) at its 45th session (1993)

Representative of the ILC in the 35th session of the Asian-African Legal Consultative Committee (AALCC) (Manila, March 1996)

Member, Working Group of the ILC on the drafting of the Statute of the International Criminal Court

Member, Drafting Committee of the ILC

Legal expert in a number of Ministerial Committees between Sudan and other countries

Member of the Legal Experts Committee of the Organization of African Unity (OAU), which formulated several regional conventions

Legal adviser in the Ministerial Councils and the Summit Conferences of the OAU (Khartoum, July 1978) (Monrovia, July 1979)

Participant in several meetings and international conferences of WHO, ILO, ITU, WIPO, Red Cross and the Executive Committee of the High Commissioner for Refugees

Member of Special Committees established for fundraising for refugees in Africa

Rapporteur of the Third Committee (Marine Scientific Research) of the summary Ninth session of the Third UN Conference on the Law of the Sea (Geneva, 1980)

Head of Sudan Delegation to the OAU Preparatory Meeting on the Draft Code of Conduct on Transfer of Technology (Addis Ababa, March 1981)

Spokesman of the African Group and the Group of 77 on all issues pertaining to Transfer of Technology, Energy, Restrictive Business Practices and Technical Co-operation among Developing Countries at the twenty-second and twenty-third sessions of the Trade and Development Board (Geneva, February and September 1981

Head of Sudan Delegation and Spokesman of the African Group and Coordinator of the Group of 77 at the fourth session of the UN Conference on the Code of Conduct on Transfer of Technology (Geneva, March-April 1981)

Spokesman of the Group of 77 on Chapter 9 (Applicable Law and Settlement of Disputes) at the UN Conference on the International Code of Conduct on Transfer of Technology (Geneva, March-April 1981)

Head of Sudan Delegation and Chairman of the Workshop on Legal Policies on Technology Transfer (Kuwait, September 1981)

Chairman of the African Group and the Group of 77 at the first session of the Intergovernmental Group of Experts on Restrictive Business Practices (Geneva, November 1981)

Chairman of the Permanent Group of 15 on Transfer and Development of Technology, within the United Nations Conference on Trade and Development (UNCTAD) (Geneva, 1980-1983)

Spokesman of the African Group and the Group of 77 at the meeting on the Economic, Commercial and Developmental

Aspects of the Industrial Property System (Geneva, February 1982)

Coordinator of the African Group and the Group of 77 at the first, second and third sessions of the Interim Committee on the International Code of Conduct on Transfer of Technology (Geneva, March, May, September-October 1982)

Coordinator of the African Group and the Group of 77 at the Meeting of Governmental Experts on the Transfer, Application and Development of Technology in the Capital Goods and Industrial Machinery Sectors (Geneva, July 1982)

Coordinator and spokesman of the African Group and the Group of 77 at the Intergovernmental Group of Experts on the Feasibility of Measuring Human Resource Flows on Reverse Transfer of Technology (Brain-Drain) (Geneva, August-September 1982)

Coordinator of developing countries on the drafting of the resolution concerning the mandate of the Office of the United Nations High Commissioner for Refugees, during the thirty-third session of the Executive Committee of the UNHCR (Geneva, October 1982)

Coordinator and spokesman of the African Group and the Group of 77 at the Meeting of Governmental Experts on the Transfer, Application and Development of Technology in the Energy Sector (Geneva, October-November 1982)

Coordinator and spokesman of the African Group and the Group of 77 at the fourth session of the Committee on Transfer of Technology (Geneva, November-December 1982)

Member, Board of Patrons, IP Management Resource (On-line version of Intellectual Property/Innovation Management Handbook), 2007

Co-President, Foreign Relations Committee, Ministry of Culture (Sudan, 2011)

President, Sudan Foundation for the defense of Syrian people (2012-2013)

Vice-President, Sudan Foundation for the defense of Rights and Freedom s (2012-2013)

Member, Sudan Foundation for Reconciliation and Religious co-existence (2012-2013)

Judicial Experience and Professional Membership of Associations

Member of the United Nations International Law Commission (ILC) (1992-1996) and (2000-2001)

Member and Chairman of several legal experts committees established within the OAU

Professor of Public International Law, University of Khartoum , Sudan

Member of the Sudan Bar Association (Khartoum)

Member of the African Jurists Association (Dakar and Paris)

Alternate Chair, Council of Foreign Relations, Ministry of Culture, Sudan

Registered Advocate and Commissioner for Oaths in the Republic of Sudan

Vice President, Sudan Organisation for the Protection of Fundamental Rights and Freedoms

Member, Sudan High Level Committee on Judicial Reform

Projects and Documents
Formulated and negotiated, on behalf of WIPO, numerous projects relating to development cooperation in the field of intellectual property

Organized, on behalf of WIPO, various seminars and workshops and presented several lectures

Drafted various documents on developmental aspects of intellectual property

Supervised and managed the administrative and substantive aspects of projects executed worldwide

Conferences, Seminars, Courses and Symposia
Represented Sudan in numerous international and regional conferences; participated in many seminars, symposia, discussion groups, and addressed graduate students on various international academic disciplines

Represented WIPO, in various international meetings, seminars and symposia

Represented WIPO on several UNDP Policy and Operations Programmes

Undertook a study tour at the Max Planck Institute (Munich) in the field of teaching of intellectual property law (1986)

Extensive lecture on COVID-19: The legal consequences of contractual obligations (May, 2020)

Publications
Euro-Arab Dialogue, June 1977

State Responsibility in International Law, September 1977

The Theory of Human Action, September 1977

The Philosophy of "Haddith" and "Sunna" in Islamic Law, January 1978

The Doctrine of Jurisdiction in International Law, December 1978

American Embassy in Tehran Case, March 1979

The Legal Regime of the Nile, December 1980

Issues pertaining to Transfer and Development of Technology in Sudan, May 1981

China and the Powers in the 19th Century, May 1981

Legal Dimensions of the Economic Cooperation among Developing Countries, June 1981

The Common Fund for Commodities, June 1981

General Aspects of Transfer of Technology at the National and International Levels, November 1981

Preferential Trading Arrangements among Developing Countries, February 1982

North-South Insurance Relations: The Unequal Exchange, December 1984

The Law of Non-Navigational Uses of International Water Courses; the International Law Commission's draft articles: An overview, November 1995

The Theory of Source and Target in Child Psychology, January 1996

A Better United Nations for the New Millennium, January 2000

Intellectual Property – A Power Tool for Economic Growth, 2003

Sudan, The Year 2020: Lessons and Visions, 2004

The Intellectual Property-Conscious Nations: Mapping the Path from Developing to Developed, 2006

Sudan 2020, (2008)

Sudan: From Least-Developed to Fast Developing, 2008

Arbitration: A Vision for the Enforcement of Justice, 2009

Arbitration: Critical Review Of Sudan Legislation onArbitration (2005), 2009

A guide to my philosophy and quotations, 2015

Sudan's Path to the Future: A realistic dream for 2025, 2017

JASTA and the third World War, 2018

A Memoir: My Nile Odyssey, 2019

How: Mind-Set Success, Promise: Nothing Less Than My Dream: 2020

My Nile Odyssey (Arabic translation): 2022

JASTA and the third World War (Arabic translation):

2022

My Nile Odyssey (Audio Book):2023

DEMYSTIFY:
The Unseen Path

Insights from Moses and Al Khidr: 2024

The Unseen Path (Arabic translation): 2025

BEYOND THE VEIL:
A METAPHYSICAL ODYSSEY: 2025

**Sudan's Marshall Plan:
Rebuilding the World's Forgotten Powerhouse: 2025**

Books under publication

WHISPERS OF POWER:
ENCOUNTERS WITH GLOBAL ICONS

VOLCANIC FURY:
THE DEADLY TOLL OF ANGER

SILENT WISDOM:
THE POWER OF SAYING NOTHING

UNIVERSE CONTROLLED:
THE SOVREIGNTY OF ALLAH

DARK SECRETS:

The HIDDEN TRUTHS

HEART's THRONE:

WHY THE MIND IS JUST A PUPPET?

Articles
A number of articles on law, economics, jurisprudence and aesthetics published in various newspapers and periodicals.

Russia's Invasion of Crimea: Is it a violation of International Law?

Index

Abraham 66, 96
Adam 71, 96
afterlife 67, 90, 99, 119
akhirah 57, 72, 90, 105
Al-Adl x, 13, 16, 63, 87, 107
Al-Alim 86
Al-Farabi 2
al-ghayb 8, 69, 102
Al-Ghazali 2
Al-Hakim x
Al-Haqq 64
Al-Hayy 86
Al-Khattab 40
Al-Qadir 87
Al-Qayyum 86
al-Qiyamah 57, 72, 90, 98, 105, 114
al-shahada 8, 102
Al-Wahid 86
Alif 73
Allah iii, v, viii, xi, 2, 5, 8, 19, 21, 27, 31, 35, 37, 43, 45, 51, 53, 58, 61, 67, 69, 75, 77, 83, 85, 91, 93, 99, 101, 107, 109, 114, 117, 122
an-Nabiyyin 96
angels iv, 30, 69, 71, 75, 102, 106
Ar-Rahim 77, 87

Ar-Rahman 16, 64, 77, 87
Arabic 13, 21
Aristotle 2

Barzakh 33, 34, 71, 72, 75, 105
barzakh 57
Basmala 77
Buddhism 2

civilizations 2, 5
commands 14, 15, 61, 62, 64, 65, 70, 75, 106
commitment 18, 42, 66, 74, 81, 91, 119, 121
communities 23, 48, 64, 94, 96, 98, 119
community 95
compassion x, 15, 16, 24, 27, 62, 65, 75, 77, 79, 81, 83, 87, 94, 95, 98, 103, 107, 111, 112, 115, 119, 121
compassionate 77, 78, 80, 83, 87, 99, 119
conduct 17, 23, 24, 54, 58, 59, 61, 63, 65, 67, 70, 72, 74, 75, 81, 83, 91, 93, 96, 103, 107, 118, 119, 121

consequences 16, 43, 57, 72, 73, 91, 95, 98, 105, 111, 114, 118, 119

cosmos iii, vii, viii, x, 1, 3, 5, 7, 12, 14, 22, 23, 32, 49, 87, 104, 118

creation iii, vi, viii, x, xi, 3, 4, 8, 10, 11, 13, 14, 16, 18, 21, 27, 31, 33, 35, 45, 51, 53, 55, 62, 63, 71, 77, 78, 80, 83, 85, 89, 101, 105, 107, 109, 115, 117, 120

creations 9

Creator iv, x, xi, 6, 18, 35, 46, 51, 59, 78, 83, 85, 87, 101, 102, 113, 115, 121

Dahr 30

David 17

death 1, 34, 57, 58, 72, 86, 105

deeds 16, 17, 24, 26, 30, 35, 40, 43, 55, 57, 58, 70, 72, 73, 90, 91, 99, 114

dimensions iii, viii, xi, 1, 5, 8, 10, 12, 13, 15, 18, 24, 27, 29, 30, 32, 34, 35, 53, 54, 65, 69, 72, 85, 101, 104, 106, 107, 109, 111, 113, 115, 118, 119

discipline iii, v, viii, x, xi, 3, 5, 12, 21, 28, 58, 59, 117

disciplined iii, x, 21, 27, 35, 46, 104

disciplines vii, viii, 56

divine iii, v, vii, xi, 2, 6, 8, 14, 16, 19, 21, 35, 37, 43, 45, 51, 53, 59, 61, 63, 65, 67, 69, 70, 72, 74, 75, 77, 83, 86, 91, 93, 100, 102, 107, 109, 115, 117, 121

duality ix, 10, 16, 38, 54

earth viii, 3, 9, 11, 14, 17, 25, 31, 32, 34, 45, 51, 63, 64, 78, 81, 88, 102, 104, 110, 111, 113, 115, 121

ecosystems 23, 46, 47, 78, 110, 118

enlightenment iv, ix, xi, 2, 28, 35, 43, 51, 59, 83, 89, 90, 94, 98, 115, 121

environment 22, 50, 111, 112

eschatological 17, 18, 26, 27, 34, 42, 43, 67, 72, 81, 90, 91, 98, 99, 114, 119

ethical x, xi, 10, 19, 23, 24, 26, 27, 39, 40, 43, 45, 49, 51, 54, 55, 58, 59, 61, 63, 65, 67, 70, 72, 74, 75, 79, 81, 83, 91, 93, 96, 98, 99, 103, 107, 109, 111, 112, 115, 118, 119, 121

ethics 66, 75, 95, 96, 107, 118

existence iii, iv, vii, xi, 1, 3, 5, 8, 12, 13, 18, 19, 25, 27, 29, 33, 34, 37, 43, 45, 51, 53, 56, 58, 59, 61, 70, 72, 75, 78, 85, 90, 96, 101, 102, 104, 106, 109, 114, 117, 119, 121

faith vii, ix, 4, 8, 11, 41, 43, 46, 49, 51, 55, 59, 66, 69, 73, 75, 77, 82, 85, 95, 99, 102, 105, 106, 118, 120, 122
fasting 23, 25, 56, 65, 88, 119
forgiveness 16, 27, 72, 79, 82, 99

Gabriel 70

Hadith 2, 40, 97
Hajj 35
Hidayah 41
Hinduism 2

ibadah 56, 64
Iblis 71
Ibrahim 66
insights iii, iv, vii, ix, xi, 1, 2, 4, 5, 7, 9, 12, 29, 46, 48, 53, 58, 66, 86, 88, 96, 97, 101, 104, 106, 120, 121
integrity x, 17, 19, 64, 66, 75, 94, 98, 119
Islam 2, 17, 79
Islamic 2, 4, 24, 37, 40, 53, 61, 63, 64, 69, 75, 77, 85, 93, 97

Jahannam 57, 73, 91, 105
Jannah 57, 73, 82, 91, 99, 105, 114
Jesus 66, 96
Jibril 70
jinn iv, 56, 69, 71, 75, 102, 103

journey iii, v, vii, xi, 1, 4, 6, 11, 12, 27, 35, 43, 51, 53, 55, 59, 83, 105, 115, 117, 119, 121
Judgment 17, 18, 26, 34, 42, 57, 67, 71, 72, 82, 90, 91, 98, 105, 114
judgment 26, 34, 72, 80
judgments 15
justice iii, v, viii, x, xi, 3, 5, 12, 19, 24, 26, 27, 32, 34, 40, 42, 43, 57, 61, 67, 72, 75, 79, 81, 83, 87, 90, 91, 95, 97, 99, 103, 105, 107, 111, 112, 114, 115, 117, 121

Kaaba 33
khalifah 111
Khatam 96
knowledge iii, viii, x, 3, 5, 11, 12, 31, 33, 49, 55, 63, 86, 89, 90, 97, 102, 106, 118, 120, 122

life iii, 1, 3, 10, 14, 15, 18, 21, 27, 29, 31, 34, 40, 43, 47, 49, 53, 56, 58, 59, 62, 67, 69, 71, 72, 74, 75, 77, 79, 81, 83, 90, 91, 93, 100, 103, 105, 106, 110, 114, 118, 120, 121
Lord 4, 9, 11, 16, 26, 30, 38, 48, 55, 71, 72, 79, 80, 82, 89, 103, 105, 112

Makaan 32

Mecca 33
Meem 73
moral ii, iii, vii, x, xi, 10, 13, 15, 16, 18, 24, 26, 27, 30, 37, 40, 43, 55, 62, 63, 65, 67, 72, 75, 77, 93, 96, 98, 99, 101, 103, 107, 111, 119
morality iv, v, 13, 23, 61, 67
Moses 42, 66, 96
mosques 33
Muhammad 42, 64, 66, 70, 79, 90, 96, 97, 118
Musa 42, 66
Muslims 77

Niyyah 40
Nizam 21
Noah 96

odyssey i, iii, iv, vi, vii, xi, 5, 12, 19, 27, 35, 43, 51, 59, 83, 115, 117, 120, 122
origin 53, 59, 61, 87, 102, 105

Paradise 41, 57, 73, 82, 91, 99, 105, 114
paradise 71
path 2, 4, 11, 12, 17, 26, 38, 41, 79, 90, 93, 98, 118, 121
perspective iv, vii, ix, 2, 7, 16, 26, 29, 30, 32, 34, 37, 39, 41, 43, 45, 49, 53, 59, 61, 67, 81, 85, 91, 93, 101, 102, 104, 106, 109, 114, 119
perspectives 2, 5
Pharaoh 42, 98
pilgrimage 33, 35
pillars vii, 17
Plato 2
power iii, iv, 1, 2, 6, 22, 25, 27, 35, 45, 46, 48, 87, 89, 90, 102, 104, 110
prayer 23, 56, 65, 69, 71, 73, 88, 89, 102, 119
prayers 23, 35
Prophet 41, 42, 66, 70, 90, 97
prophet 96

Qadar 31, 39
qadar 102
Quran iii, iv, vi, xi, 2, 5, 7, 18, 21, 27, 29, 34, 37, 43, 45, 51, 53, 58, 61, 67, 69, 75, 77, 83, 85, 91, 93, 107, 109, 114, 117, 121
Quranic iii, iv, viii, ix, xi, 2, 3, 7, 10, 13, 17, 21, 26, 27, 29, 30, 32, 34, 35, 37, 40, 45, 46, 49, 53, 54, 59, 61, 67, 69, 75, 80, 85, 88, 90, 93, 101, 104, 106, 107, 109, 112, 115, 119

rahmah 63, 94, 112
Ramadan 24, 65

Satan 71
soul iii, v, vii, xi, 15, 25, 34, 40, 53, 59, 63, 102, 105, 117, 119
souls 34, 57, 71, 72, 90, 105
Spirit 30
spiritual iii, iv, vii, xi, 3, 5, 11, 12, 18, 19, 23, 25, 27, 28, 30, 33, 35, 40, 41, 45, 46, 49, 51, 53, 59, 63, 65, 66, 74, 80, 82, 83, 85, 88, 91, 93, 99, 101, 103, 105, 106, 113, 115, 117, 121
spirituality iii, 29, 50, 53, 58, 69, 77, 93, 96, 100

transcend ix, 11, 121
transcendence 3
transcendent 85, 87
transcends iii, 1, 5, 7, 10, 21, 30, 34, 35, 38, 53, 54, 56, 61, 70, 86
transformation 34, 42, 98, 121
transformative 34, 90, 91, 120
transgress 111
transgressed 16, 27, 79
tribulations 41
truth viii, 1, 4, 5, 9, 10, 16, 18, 25, 26, 30, 32, 38, 55, 64, 88, 89, 103, 104
truths iii, iv, ix, 5, 8, 12, 63, 121

unity viii, 23, 32, 33, 85, 86, 88, 109, 110, 113, 115, 117, 118

universe iii, v, vii, xi, 1, 5, 7, 11, 13, 14, 19, 21, 23, 26, 27, 29, 32, 33, 38, 45, 85, 88, 101, 102, 109, 110, 117

Veil iii, iv, vii, ix, xi, 117, 120, 121
veil i, iii, iv, 5, 121
vision xi, 12, 17, 22, 26, 34, 42, 67, 72, 81, 90, 114, 119

wisdom iii, iv, x, xi, 3, 5, 11, 13, 18, 22, 25, 27, 32, 33, 35, 37, 39, 41, 43, 45, 51, 56, 62, 73, 75, 82, 87, 88, 90, 93, 94, 97, 101, 104, 106, 109, 110, 112, 113, 115, 120, 121

Yawm 57, 72, 90, 98, 105, 114

zakah 23, 80
zakat 17, 56, 65

www.ingramcontent.com/pod-product-compliance
Lightning Source LLC
LaVergne TN
LVHW051556080426
835510LV00020B/3007